PRAISE FOR

She Come By It Natural

"Like Parton herself, Smarsh's treatment is so much deeper than what appears on the surface. . . . Smarsh tells Parton's story through the eyes of women who grew up in rural America struggling to make ends meet. . . . A new generation is just now realizing the power of Parton's music. Some certainly will find out about it because of Smarsh's book, which tells Parton's story and puts it into step with our times."

—*The Spokane Spokesman-Review*

"Smarsh explains that Parton's full legacy is much deeper and more rewarding than it might seem from casual listening."

—*The Pitch* podcast

"Throughout the book, Parton and Smarsh are in unspoken dialogue with one another, sharing common language and struggle through the beauty of country music."

—*Willamette Week*

"Dolly comes vividly to life in [the book's] pages . . . a serious, not worshipful but something better, deeply respectful critical portrait . . . She really is as sharp and as complicated as we'd begun to suspect."

—*Shawangunk Journal*

"We will always love reading about Dolly Parton."

—*Yahoo! Life*

"*She Come By It Natural* will appeal to a wide range of readers who are curious about Parton. Smarsh finds a sweet spot between biography and memoir that lets her move nimbly between her personal affection for Parton's impact on women's lives and her journalistic analysis of Parton's artistry, business acumen, and iconic role in our quick-changing zeitgeist."

—Chapter 16

"Sarah Smarsh expertly explores the overlooked social contributions of women. . . . [An] inspiring tribute to Dolly Parton herself."

—CNN.com

"*She Come By It Natural* is the latest—and best, and most affecting and convincing—component of what appears to be, at long last, the Great Dolly Parton Renaissance."

—*The Ringer*

"A love letter both to Parton and to the women who continue to see themselves in her songs."

—*Shelf Awareness*

"[Smarsh] skillfully illustrat[es] how [Parton's] music speaks to women, especially those from a lower-class background."

—Bookreporter

"Smarsh seamlessly weaves her family's experiences with Parton's biography—triumphs and shortcomings alike—and cultural context. *She Come By It Natural* is, as a result, a relatable examination of one of country music's brightest stars and an inspiring tale of what women can learn from one another."

—*BookPage*

ALSO BY SARAH SMARSH

Heartland

SHE COME

=== BY IT ===

NATURAL

Dolly Parton and the Women
Who Lived Her Songs

Sarah Smarsh

Scribner

New York   London   Toronto   Sydney   New Delhi

Scribner
An Imprint of Simon & Schuster, Inc.
1230 Avenue of the Americas
New York, NY 10020

First Scribner trade paperback edition September 2021

SCRIBNER and design are registered trademarks of The Gale Group, Inc.,
used under license by Simon & Schuster, Inc., the publisher of this work.

For information about special discounts for bulk purchases,
please contact Simon & Schuster Special Sales at 1-866-506-1949 or
business@simonandschuster.com.

The Simon & Schuster Speakers Bureau can bring authors to your
live event. For more information or to book an event, contact the
Simon & Schuster Speakers Bureau at 1-866-248-3049 or
visit our website at www.simonspeakers.com.

Interior design by Erika R. Genova

Manufactured in the United States of America

10   9   8   7   6   5   4   3   2

Library of Congress Cataloging-in-Publication Data has been applied for.

ISBN 978-1-9821-5728-9
ISBN 978-1-9821-5729-6 (pbk)
ISBN 978-1-9821-5730-2 (ebook)

For Grandma Betty

FOREWORD

If you doubt that women have advanced much during the century since they gained the right to vote in 1920, consider the present-day phenomenon that is Dolly Parton.

She adorns female torsos as a T-shirt, declaring power not with the term "feminist" but with a big ol' pile of hair. She burns on desks as a blasphemous prayer candle, her image canonized with a halo (above a big ol' pile of hair). Well into her seventies, she frequently holds forth on talk shows and awards-ceremony stages, where women of a certain age historically have gone unseen.

People can't get enough of Dolly, who is now—as hagiographic magazine pieces, breathless tweets, and diverse, roaring audiences attest—a universally beloved icon recognized as a creative genius with a goddess-sized heart.

Not so long ago, she was best known by many people as the punch line of a boob joke.

Why, then, this new shift in regard?

When Parton was born into rural poverty in 1946, women's suffrage had been granted by US constitutional amendment just twenty-six years prior. Women had recently made economic strides amid a wartime economy but still were widely abused by a system in which the female body had few protections from assault, unwanted pregnancy, or undervalued labor. Women in poverty and women of color fared the worst, on the losing end of societal structures favoring wealth and whiteness. Meanwhile, their contributions toward gender equality went unnoticed, undocumented, and ill-understood.

By the 1960s, young Parton—short on book-learnin' but long on smarts—left her Appalachian holler with independent dreams that defied gender norms. Like so many women of her generation, she got the job done, breaking free from the shackles of men's income, men's decisions, men's anything. And also like so many, she was woefully underestimated and undervalued along the way.

While she was offered as a smiling "girl singer" at the outset of her career and referenced foremost by her physical attributes for decades to come, Parton was a brilliant force—not just in songwriting and singing but in gender performance and business. Many of her twenty-first-century fans are thus "discovering" what was there all along, in plain sight but for the blinders of patriarchy: Parton's artistry, intellectual depth, and self-fashioned paradoxes that slyly comment on our country's long-denied caste system (looking "cheap," say, while by all accounts acting with pure class).

There is about the current Dolly fervor, I sense, an apology among some for the lifelong slut-shaming: I had no idea she was all those things. Now I understand. Now I see better. Parton projected a sweetly defiant self-possession throughout her career in a man's world; one doesn't get the impression that she expected or cared whether such validation would come. But it's a magnificent thing to witness—an atonement countless women have deserved but never received, flowering while the woman is alive to see it.

Like Dolly, I grew up on a struggling family farm (albeit with indoor plumbing). My hard luck, like Dolly's, was mixed with the unjust advantage of white skin and the chance fortune of a strong mind. But the palms of my hands were red and swollen, cut by stems of invasive ryegrass that I pulled from our wheat fields before summer harvest, and the difficult but beautiful world I knew was dying in the cogs of industrial economies.

I was a reader, when I could get ahold of something to read, and literature showed me places I'd never seen. Another art form, though, showed me my own place: country music. Its sincere lyrics and familiar accent confirmed, with triumph and sorrow, that my home—invisible or ridiculed elsewhere in news and popular culture—deserved to be known, and that it was complicated and good.

I grew up to sometimes inhabit more cosmopolitan places and found around me a common refrain about music: "I like everything except country." (Or, sometimes, "I like everything except country and rap.") If someone did like a country song or musician, this information required a qualifier: "I don't like country music, but I do like Johnny Cash." The snickering summary of the genre, among those who didn't know it firsthand: "My pickup truck broke down and my dawg and my woman left me." (A classist dismissal not unlike, perhaps, racist dismissals of rap music.) "It all sounds the same," people told me, proving nothing but their ignorance.

So, in 2016, when I heard about a new fellowship to commission extensive writing on the intersection of roots music and culture for the small but excellent *No Depression* magazine, I jumped at the chance. I'd already been doing research for a piece of writing about Parton's reemergence that election year, during which she was touring with a new record, as a unifying balm for a country freshly torn by social upheaval. Political headlines were fixating on a hateful, sexist version of rural, working-class America that I did not recognize. Dolly's music and life contained what I wanted to say about class, gender, and my female forebears: That country music by women was the formative feminist text of my life.

Parton does not identity as a "feminist" and, like me, comes from a place where "theory" is a solid guess about how the coyotes keep getting into the chicken house. Her decades-long tendency to perform while wearing all white is not, I am certain, a nod to suffragists. But her work is a nod to women who can't afford to travel to the march, women working with their bodies while others are tweeting with their fingers.

The journalism fellowship offered twenty-five cents per word for what would be a yearlong effort—a poverty wage and far less than I'd earned a decade prior for writing easy airline-magazine features. (Such is the post-digital economic state of journalism.) I was already under deadline with a major publishing house for a book that I knew might be my life's work, *Heartland*. There was nothing sensible, for little pay and a niche magazine's small readership, about spending a year concurrently writing about Dolly Parton. I submitted my application.

One month before the 2016 presidential election, I learned that I'd won the fellowship, funded by the FreshGrass Foundation. My work would be published by *No Depression* as a four-part, print-only series over the course of 2017. The moment in which the writing emerged—outlined just before the first Women's March, completed just before the mainstream explosion of the #MeToo movement—is palpable in these pages.

Now, amid a political climate that is still roiling, points on gender and economic status remain timely. But this story is about much more than that. It's about leaving home but never really leaving home. It's about an unfashionable quality in our angry society—grace—and its ability to inspire the best in others. It's also about a seventy-year-old woman telling a hot young cowboy to dance in place while she plays the fiddle.

Since completing this deeply researched work in its original form, I have come across previously published texts that make similar conclusions about country music and Dolly Parton—unknown to me while I was writing but in harmony all the same: Nadine Hubbs's 2014 book *Rednecks, Queers, & Country Music*, a 2014 *BUST* cover story, even a 1987 issue of *Ms.* in which Parton was named one of the magazine's women of the year and Gloria Steinem wrote the tribute to her. Independent emergence of like ideas underscores their importance and validity; meanwhile, I aimed to ensure that any idea that was not my original thought is clearly attributed to its source. The contents are slightly revised from their original serial format, in part to create the seamless read a book requires. Time references have not been edited (i.e., changing "last summer" to "four years ago"), preserving a snapshot of a critical moment in America. It's a snapshot that I know to have been heavily consulted and directly drawn from by national media, including a hit podcast on which I appeared as a guest.

On that 2019 podcast, *Dolly Parton's America*, host Jad Abumrad presents Parton with my take on her brand of feminism, a term she had rejected outright in their previous interview.

"We went back to Dolly one more time, and I took that question that I asked her and reframed it in light of something that we had seen and that Sarah Smarsh had told us," Abumrad narrates. "That there are the feminists in theory, but there are also the feminists in practice."

"That's the one. That's me. That's me," Parton replied ". . . I think that's a good way of saying it. I live it. I work it. And I think there's power in it for me."

Power, indeed. Unlike most celebrities, while the world fell apart in 2020, Parton somehow only became more relevant.

Were I writing this book today, therefore, some of the particulars would be different. Then, the crisis for which Parton provided aid was a historic wildfire in the Great Smoky Mountains; now, it's a catastrophic pandemic of global proportions. At the start of the

Covid-19 outbreak, Parton donated a million dollars to Vanderbilt University's research of the virus—research that led to development of a highly effective vaccine from pharmaceutical company Moderna. (This poignant turn of events—Parton literally saved the world—sent Dolly Mania to new heights.)

Then, the race controversy in Parton's immediate midst concerned her dinner-theater tourist attraction, the decades-old Dixie Stampede, which presented the Civil War as silly, whitewashed entertainment; in response to criticism, in 2018 the Parton-owned business dropped "Dixie" from its name and moved away from the Civil War conceit. Now, after video of George Floyd's murder at the hands of law enforcement in May 2020 ignited worldwide protests against police brutality and systemic racism, the pervasive Black Lives Matter movement is forcing a national reckoning in public policy and beyond—presenting celebrities with a choice about how to wield their cultural influence.

Many country music stars expressed solidarity in the wake of Floyd's death. Faith Hill, for instance, called for removal of the Confederate "stars and bars" from the state flag of her native Mississippi, as protesters toppled monuments to slave holders across the country. And another business dropped the term "Dixie": the platinum-selling trio the Dixie Chicks, who as "The Chicks" released a bold protest anthem and accompanying video of triumphant demonstrators for Black Lives Matter and other progressive causes. Amid all this, Parton, who previously made no direct statement supporting the #MeToo movement or any other political uprising over the decades, initially stayed quiet.

During the summer of 2020, though, in a cover story for *Billboard*, she surprised some fans—not with the content of her thoughts but with the fact that she spelled them out in no uncertain terms: "Of course Black lives matter," Parton said, her lack of trademark equivocation perhaps revealing that the issue is at its core not just political but moral. "Do we think our little white asses are the only ones that matter? No!" (Country-bred readers might wonder whether the interviewer misheard "lily-white asses.")

As Confederate monuments came down across the South, petitions grew for Tennessee to erect a monument to their favorite daughter. In early 2021, the state legislature considered a bill, with rare bipartisan support, to do just that—until Parton herself asked lawmakers to drop it. "Given all that is going on in the world," she said after expressing her thanks in a statement, "I don't think putting me on a pedestal is appropriate at this time. I hope, though, that somewhere down the road several years from now or perhaps after I'm gone if you still feel I deserve it, then I'm certain I will stand proud in our great State Capitol as a grateful Tennessean. In the meantime, I'll continue to try to do good work to make this great state proud." Many noted the irony that the qualities of her statement are precisely why folks want to give her a statue. (As it happens, some years ago I wrote about just such a statue—at the end of this book.)

Plenty else has changed since my writing. Then, Parton's most recent TV foray was an NBC Christmas movie inspired by one of her hit songs; now, it's a Netflix series inspired by several of her hit songs.

Then, Parton's Imagination Library had donated 80 million books to children around the world; now, the number is well past 150 million. Then, I included another writer's brilliant argument that rapper Nicki Minaj had much in common with Parton; now, I'd note the Parton-esque qualities of cross-genre star Lizzo.

Dolly's Grammy count has increased, and my regard for Roseanne Barr—whose television character I portrayed as a working-class feminist hero and who subsequently made vile, racist public comments—has greatly diminished.

I would lament insufficient attention to female artists in the 2019 Ken Burns documentary *Country Music* but celebrate that such a series was finally made. I'd observe the overt, intersectional feminism and racial statements of country acts that have since emerged, such as Our Native Daughters, Mickey Guyton, and the Highwomen.

I would write about not just one female candidate for president but several, representing multiple races, ethnicities, and regions in the 2020 primary election. None of them made it to the general election as contenders for the top spot, Hillary Clinton's 2016 loss of which I document here, but they all made history.

I would observe that more than a few abusive, powerful men have fallen—fired by the corporate world they ran, some even sent to prison—thanks to the courage of women who shouted their names.

The world has transformed in the last few years. But the big themes and arguments here abide. At least one detail does, too: A study published last year found that, in keeping with a 2016 statistic I cited, songs performed by female artists still accounted for just 10 percent of country radio plays in 2019.

Readers of my previous work as journalist, essayist, and author will recognize Grandma Betty, who was born just months apart from Dolly. Several *Heartland* readers have told me that their biggest laugh from the book was Betty's serious request to me in the mid-1990s, when I was a teenager and she was considering her mortality, that I make sure she be buried without a bra. "I hate the damn things," she told me. "You can burn 'em when I die."

She soon beat me to it. After her professional retirement that decade, she threw all her underwire bras and pantyhose onto our farm's burn pile, where we dumped trash, and doused them with lighter fluid.

Like Dolly, Betty doesn't call herself a feminist. She wasn't considering the inaccurate trope about second-wave feminists ceremoniously burning their brassieres in protest. Intending to dress comfortably in her retirement years, she simply had no further use for the things and wanted to watch the straps turn to ash. I suspect that she also, modestly and pragmatically, didn't want her undergarments blowing from the trash pile into the nearby work shed, hay barn, or pig pen. So Grandma lit a smoke and flung the match, and her bras caught fire in the Kansas wind.

It's the kind of thing you could write a country song about.

—*Sarah Smarsh,*
March 2021

PART ONE

DOLLY PARTON EMBODIES THE
WORKING WOMAN'S FIGHT

PART ONE

DOLLY PARTON EMBODIES THE
WORKING WOMAN'S FIGHT

When Dolly Parton's holiday movie about crises and miracles in East Tennessee, *Christmas of Many Colors*, premiered on television last November, wildfires were burning up the Great Smoky Mountains where she first strummed a guitar. As smoke cleared in Parton's native Sevier County, the death toll would reach fourteen. Tennessee governor Bill Haslam told the *New York Times* it was the biggest fire in the state in a century.

Hours before the film aired, Parton announced that her Dollywood Foundation would give a thousand dollars per month for six months to every family who lost their home. About nine hundred families would apply for the funds.

When I posted news of Parton's fire-victim fund to social media that evening, a West Virginia acquaintance and filmmaker who documents poverty in Appalachia commented, "My first words after the fires: Dolly will save 'em." As she typed this, 11.5 million people were tuning in to see Parton make a cameo appearance in *Christmas of Many Colors*—as a generous sex worker shunned by self-proclaimed Christians in her hometown.

Much has been sung about auburn-haired "Jolene," the real-life siren Parton says worked at a bank and flirted with her husband when he came in to do business; she inspired the most covered of her hundreds of original recorded songs. But the woman to whom music owes much more is the blond "town tramp" Parton admired as a child. Parton created her look in that woman's image.

She had "yellow hair piled on top of her head, red lipstick, her eyes all painted up, and her clothes all tight and flashy," Parton recalled in a 2016 interview with *Southern Living*. "I just thought she was the prettiest thing I'd ever seen. And then when everybody said, 'Oh, she's just trash,' I thought, 'That's what I'm going to be when I grow up! Trash!'"

Parton, now seventy-one, has told this story many times because she is a woman whose appearance provokes people to demand an explanation. In *Christmas of Many Colors*, she finally pays full homage to the "painted lady" by making her the guardian angel of a narrative based loosely on a Christmas during Parton's childhood.

In the movie, young Dolly stands on a sidewalk strumming a guitar on a cold December night while holiday shoppers bustle along the main street of her tiny hometown; she's trying to help her dad and siblings come up with $69.95, plus tax, to finally get her mom a gold wedding band. The yellow-haired woman, in her tight clothes and high heels, drops a twenty-dollar bill into Dolly's guitar case—but a self-righteous shopkeeper sweeping the sidewalk refuses to let the elated child keep money tainted by the woman's sins.

"You get away from her," the outraged woman chides. "Why, this is a child of God. She don't want your dirty money." Before she sweeps her broom at the woman, she adds, "Comin' around decent folks all painted up, sticking out everywhere."

"Boy, you and that broom make a good team, you ol' witch," Parton's character replies before she clicks off into the darkness with an apology to young Dolly that she couldn't give her the money.

This signature Parton trifecta—eyebrow-raising tight clothes, generosity of heart, and a take-no-crap attitude—is an overlooked, unnamed sort of feminism I recognize in the hard-luck women who raised me. They didn't sell their bodies, but they faced scorn for where they came from. Most of them left school in ninth, tenth, eleventh grade. There was no feminist literature or theory in our lives. There was only life, in which we were women—economically disenfranchised, working on our feet in restaurants and factories, and hopelessly sexualized.

When I was a kid in the 1980s, my mom's long red acrylic

fingernails didn't slow her down driving a UPS truck, dragging and pushing boxes of Christmas presents she and her own family wouldn't receive. Her other job was applying makeup for middle-class women at a department-store counter in a Wichita mall, a male manager stopping by to adjust the metal name tag pinned to her blouse. She knew exactly what was going on and neither liked it nor complained, the latter being risky business for a woman who must keep her job. She knew that the only way a woman with no money or connections can beat the game—that is to say, pay the bills for herself and her children—is by playing it.

In her songwriting, movie roles, and stage persona, Parton's exaltation of the strengths of this frequently vilified class of American woman is at once the greatest self-aware gender performance in modern history and a sincere expression of who Parton is. She stands for the poor woman, the working-class woman whose feminine sexuality is often an essential device for survival and yet whose tough presence might be considered "masculine" in corners of society where women haven't always worked, where the archaic concept of a "lady" lingers. They are single mothers in need of welfare and abortions, females without diplomas but possessing strong opinions, complicated people reduced to a "backwards" stereotype in the media. Long shamed as a moral scourge in the US, they have precious few ambassadors to convey their grace.

What Parton has accomplished for feminism has less to do with feminism than it has to do with Parton, and she has everything to do with rural poverty. As my grandma would say about what alchemized a future legend in those Appalachian hills in the middle of the twentieth century, she come by it natural.

OUTTA THAT HOLLER

The fourth of twelve siblings, Parton was born on a small farm in 1946; her father, Lee, paid the doctor a bag of grain for the delivery. As those familiar with her music know, growing up wearing dresses made of feed sacks didn't make her sorrowful but rather grateful—a fact that, paradoxically, has helped make her a very rich woman. The royalties for "Coat of Many Colors," her enduring 1971 song about cherishing a garment her mother sewed from rags in spite of being shamed for it at school, roll in year after year.

Of her many hits, Parton has described that tribute to her mother, Avie Lee, as the one most special to her. She says she got her musical talent from that side of her family, whom she describes as "dreamers." During Parton's childhood, radios, record players, and electricity hadn't yet reached the rural poor, and they entertained themselves in their own homes with old ways passed down from European country peasantry. Her maternal grandfather, a Pentecostal preacher, played fiddle and wrote songs.

Avie Lee's brother, Billy, played guitar and noticed young Dolly's musical talent. He helped get her onto the Knoxville radio and TV show *Cas Walker's Farm and Home Hour*. Billy reportedly bought Dolly her first proper guitar, a child-sized acoustic Martin, when she was eight (replacing the one she'd made from an old mandolin and two found strings). He helped her write her first single, "Puppy Love," penned when she was eleven and recorded in 1959, when she was thirteen, after a thirty-hour bus ride to Goldband Records in Lake Charles, Louisiana, with her grandma.

By that time, rock and roll—rooted in Southern Black culture—was sweeping white America and infusing country sounds. It showed up in the up-tempo dance beat of "Puppy Love" and in Uncle Billy's slick Elvis-style pompadour. Parton admired rockabilly pioneer Rose Maddox, the daughter of Alabama sharecroppers. But Appalachia's ancient melodies, the poor European cousin to slavery's African blues, were the songs that shaped her first. In one hit from her early career, "Apple Jack," which she has said portrays a composite of real people, she tells of visiting a mountain-music man who gifted her his banjo when he died—a bit of Africa that had reached East Tennessee over the centuries.

While Parton's musicianship and mentorship came from

her mother's family, her business acumen, she says, came from her father—a tenderhearted lifelong laborer who didn't learn to read and write but nonetheless was savvy with a horse trade and could stretch a bit of money a long way. The sharp business mind that eventually built an empire worth hundreds of millions of dollars was also influenced by the premium her dad put on their humble home.

She described those seemingly conflicting interests—"getting out" and being where you most belong—onstage in Kansas City during her 2016 tour for her latest album, *Pure and Simple*. That production stripped away the razzle-dazzle of backup bands and big sets featured on so many of her tours, putting Parton on a mostly bare stage with three backup musicians and a few cascades of white fabric. The show started with the sound of crickets and bulbs blinking like lightning bugs.

At one point during the performance, Parton climbed a few steps to sit on a white platform described as a front porch but that turned out to be an elevated position for communing with heaven. Before singing "Smoky Mountain Memories," her 1978 song about poor workers drawn north during the midcentury factory boom, she paid tribute to her father's hard work, economic decisions, and commitment to his family.

"Lee, you oughta go up'air, get them kids outta that

holler," she remembered people telling her dad. But after a short stint in Detroit when Dolly was a child, Lee announced that he would die in the East Tennessee mountains. They wouldn't have much there, he knew, but they'd have food and shelter—and they'd be home.

Parton stood up with a flute to open the number. She couldn't sit while she performed it, she said, because her dad deserved a standing ovation. In an instant, thousands of people stood up—her audiences would do the Hokey Pokey if she asked—and Parton laughed.

"Not from you!" she said, and the crowd laughed with her. Then they sat down and cried while she sang.

Turning her attention to Avie Lee, Parton set up "Coat of Many Colors" with analogous tales of her mother's creativity in the face of deprivation. To boost the kids' spirits, Parton recalled, Avie would send them outside to pick the best rock for her to cook "stone soup"—always intending to select and praise the child who had the hardest day.

One imagines Parton, who told the crowd her family had running water "if we ran and got it," absorbed her wit and natural poetry from her mother's language. "If we had some ham, we'd have ham and eggs—if we had some eggs," Parton quoted her mom to the crowd.

Parton has repeated such anecdotes for decades—mind you, she spent eighteen years in her parents' cabin, compared with more than half a century in Nashville and beyond, most of which she has lived at the height of fame and fortune. But fans who have heard it a thousand times gladly line up to hear it a thousand and one, maybe because there are so few entertainers who truly own such experiences. You can recognize that owner-ship by its humor.

Joking about poverty is a hallmark of women in poor spaces, while more privileged people tend to regard it with precious sadness—a demonstration of their own sense of guilt, perhaps, or lack of understanding about what brings happiness. Firsthand experience allows for a tale that's more complex than a somber lament. Those women never had to feign being impressed by things their husbands couldn't afford to give them, and in that gulf between one's reality and the middle-class images in magazine advertisements arises a dry humor.

When my grandma recounted my biological grandfather's proposal to her when she became pregnant with my mother at age sixteen, for instance, it was with a laugh and a cigarette drag.

"It wasn't any of this, 'please be my darling wife.' Sheeeeit," she said, and we both cracked up—not at our own family's misfortunes but at the delusions of women who got a sentimental proposal and a big diamond before they spent a lifetime pushing a vacuum.

If you don't find that edge in Parton's work, you haven't listened to much of it. Recurring motifs of her early songs, in particular, include hypocritical, violent, and even murderous men; women being used, neglected, and shamed; and dying children. (The baby sibling Parton was charged with caring for as a child got sick and died.) Known for her "fake" appearance—the wigs, the synthetic fabrics clinging to a surgically altered body, the acrylic nails in pastel shades— Parton can be a very dark realist when she writes. That darkness in a woman's voice, plain stories of hell on earth sung by women who have little to carry them forward but faith, is the divine feminine of American roots music.

"Little Sparrow," from her 2001 album by the same name, blends the bluegrass, folk, and country gospel sounds of her native home and is sung in the voice of a jilted, devastated woman warning young girls to "never trust the hearts of men." As haunting as the melody is, Parton—who is given to undercutting serious moments with an endearing bit of nervous humor—sets it up with a joke onstage: "I call it my little sad-ass song."

Parton says you can't be from where she's from and not like woeful melodies. The worst stories she tells of those mountains in her songwriting seem to represent what she saw outside her family's house. The biggest grievance she has discussed about her childhood is that her father wouldn't say "I love you"—a common cultural affliction for men of all classes in that period and, perhaps to a lesser degree, still today. But Parton insists that, in practice, her home was so rich in love that every material poverty was mitigated.

After the moving tribute to her musical mother and industrious father, at another stop on the same tour—in Austin, Texas—Parton made her way down the steps of the "porch" before it was wheeled offstage.

"Time to come down from heaven, I reckon," she said, and a muscular, bare-armed man in a black vest and hat previously introduced as her "sexy cowboy" carried out a new instrument. (By this point, she had played guitar, dulcimer, and flute.) It was white and covered in rhinestones, like all her other instruments, including a grand piano she played for one number.

"Oh, the cowboy brought me a banjo," Parton said. Soon she was shredding on it with her talon fingernails during "Rocky Top," a bluegrass song exalting the Tennessee hills. It was written in 1967 by a married pair of innkeepers just up the road from Parton's hometown in Gatlinburg, the place hardest hit by the recent wildfires.

During the bridge, Parton slung the banjo over her back, and the cowboy handed her a fiddle. While the fast beat pulsed and one of her band members played another banjo, Parton tapped the air with her bow like a conductor. Right before her solo, she pointed the bow at the cowboy and said in time with the rhythm, "You dance." The sexy cowboy hooked his thumbs into the belt loops of his tight jeans and kicked up his heels in place while she fiddled and the crowd roared.

Parton spends more time than the average performer onstage deferring to others with what, by all known accounts, is a sincere humility—praising the crowd, thanking her own band, honoring her family and her roots. But at that moment in the show, tears still wet on faces after the poignant songs for mama and daddy, it was Parton's own delight, desires, and power on display. She sang the song, she played two instruments on the song, and the hot piece of man next to her was on her payroll. When she said "dance," he danced.

Sex was the third formative pillar of her life alongside music and religion, Parton said in her 1994 autobiography, *My Life and Other Unfinished Business*. Growing up, she used to haunt an abandoned chapel with broken windows and buckled floorboards where teenagers left condom wrappers under the porch; inside was a defunct piano and "dirty drawings" on the walls. In that space of music, sex, and God, Parton wrote, she experienced a spiritual epiphany that "it was all right for me to be a sexual being." Indeed, she has described herself as having been hormonally precocious both inside and out.

While famously lifted, nipped, and tucked over the years, her figure was just as improbable as it naturally developed.

The resulting attention from males clued her in to her own sexual power at a young age, and she embraced it, dyeing her lips with iodine from the family medicine cabinet for lack of lipstick. This zeal for sexy behavior did not, in the eyes of her people's strict patriarchal religion, honor her father and her mother.

In a 2003 *Rolling Stone* interview, she described her father punishing her for making herself up. " 'This is my natural color!' " she remembered insisting. "The more Daddy tried to rub it off, the redder it was. It's like, 'This red ass of yours after a whipping, is that your natural color?' Oh, I got lots of whippin's over makeup."

Her mom and preacher grandpa shuddered, too, worried that the devil had led Dolly down Jezebel's path. During her 1983 television special *Dolly in London*, Parton called herself "the original punk rocker." In the early sixties, as a teen, she pierced her own ears to hang feathers from them and ratted her hair. When her mother suggested she'd been possessed, Parton told her to give credit where it was due—not to Satan but to Dolly herself.

"I couldn't get my hair big enough or 'yaller' enough, couldn't get my skirt tight enough, my blouses low enough," she recalled in her autobiography. ". . . Of course, I had to get away from home to really put on the dog. I'd go into the four-for-a-quarter picture booth at Woolworth's, unbutton my blouse, push my headlights up with my arms and take pictures."

What women who didn't grow up on a farm might miss is that, where Parton was from, this common act of female adolescent rebellion wasn't just about attracting boys. It was about claiming her femininity in a place where everyone, male and female alike, summoned "masculine" attributes and downplayed "feminine" ones in order to survive.

"My sisters and I used to cling desperately to anything halfway feminine," Parton wrote. "We could see the pictures of the models in the newspapers that lined the walls of our house and the occasional glimpse we would get at a magazine. We wanted to look like them. They didn't look at all like they had to work in the fields. They didn't look like they had to take a spit bath in a dishpan."

For Parton, lipstick and store-bought clothing represented not just a life beyond backbreaking labor but also a level of economic agency that might protect a woman from assault. Indeed, research indicates that impoverished women are at higher risk of experiencing severe male violence.

"Womanhood was a difficult thing to get a grip on in those hills, unless you were a man," Parton wrote. "[Glamorous women in magazines] didn't look as if men and boys could just put their hands on them anytime they felt like it, and with any degree of roughness they chose. The way they looked, if a man wanted to touch them, he'd better be damned nice to them."

Women of all classes suffer male violence. Still, there's a hard truth to Parton's view. In the social climb to come, she had white skin, good health, and loads of talent on her side. But something the world values even less than a girl is a poor one.

My family's poverty was nothing like Parton's, but it was enough that I knew shame. We lived in rural Kansas, so I didn't feel it until I started school, where other children's clothes and lives were there for me to see and contrast with my own.

That reckoning began even before I reached the school on the first day: The bus pulled up to our long dirt driveway, and I climbed on with a paper grocery sack full of supplies. I had been in a state of bliss as my mother checked off the teacher-provided list she had in her purse with a small calculator and her plastic coupon organizer. But I was the only child on the bus whose supplies weren't in a backpack, and by the time we reached the school—nearly an hour-long drive after all the necessary stops, winding along dirt roads and ruts—I was embarrassed when I unloaded the new crayons and pencils I prized from a paper sack.

If you're a peaceful child, as I was, not given to throwing tantrums to process frustration, in such moments you have two choices: hang your head and cry or tilt your chin up and let the tears inside you turn into a salty form of power. The women I knew had taught me the latter skill— a particular strength for a female in that she will be called upon throughout her life to not only care for herself but also to care for others. Little room is left in such a life for one's own complaints.

The transmutation of pain into power is a feature of all musical genres and indeed all forms of art. For women in poverty, though, it is not just a song but a way of life, not just a performance but a necessity. As with Loretta Lynn, Tammy Wynette, Patsy Cline, and so many female country performers before and since, Parton's music expresses this.

Her special twist, unlike most of the rest, is that she conveys it with palpable positivity and a smile— understanding so deeply the connection between a difficult past and a blessed present that her mission on stage and in life is to honor that tension in other people's lives.

She reminds her audiences that, no matter where they came from, everyone can identify with being shamed one way or another, and no one deserves it. Never be ashamed of your home, your family, yourself, your religion, she says, and adoring crowds applaud. One need look no further than her immense LGBTQ following to know that Parton's trans-formation from a slut-shamed, talented teenage bumpkin to entertainment superstar contains a universal struggle that has less to do with being Appalachian than with being human. If her presence and the appreciation it instills in people could be whittled to a phrase, it's "be what you are."

In order to deliver that message to the masses, though—in order to tell the stories of the impoverished women where she was from—Parton would have to be the woman who left behind both poverty and place. That meant leaving the people she loved most, but it wasn't a tough decision.

In her autobiography she described going to see a traveling sideshow as a child and being stunned to recognize her cousin Myrtle made up to play the "alligator girl."

"I could understand her completely," Parton wrote. "After all, I wanted to leave the mountains too, and I wanted attention. She probably thought I was making fun or blowing her cover, but I just wanted to say, 'Hello, I understand. Be the alligator girl. Be whatever your dreams and your luck will let you be.'"

Parton's dreams involved music, of course. She practiced on her guitar, put an empty tin can on a stick wedged between the boards of her family's front porch and performed for chickens. But her dreams also involved stardom. To that end, it doesn't matter how well you play and sing if you're only doing it on your own front porch.

Luckily, Uncle Billy had a car. The driver's-side door was

wired to keep it on the frame, so that he had to crawl in and out of the passenger side, but the car moved. Over the years, he'd drive Parton two hundred miles east to Nashville to knock on doors. Record executives turned them away, and they slept in his car—the next day always driving back to the farm, back to Sevier County.

TALKING THROUGH SONGS

A few years ago, Parton dedicated a room of photos and memorabilia at Dollywood, the theme park she opened in her home county in 1986, to Bill Owens. In a video recording viewed by many of the park's 3 million annual visitors, Parton sings a song to her uncle Billy from a small screen.

In the song, she recalls the two of them after chores were done dreaming of a world far beyond those hills, and his instruction: how to pick, how to yodel, how to shake her fears, how to act in proper company. "You told me I was special," she sings, "and I took it to heart." With the chorus, she plainly states "I love you" over and over, the words her dad couldn't say and that Billy might have struggled with, too.

In part because of that Tennessee man's loving tutelage, though, Parton is now the most successful female artist in country music history. She has sold well over 100 million albums and is a member of the Songwriters Hall of Fame; since 1964, she has published more than three thousand songs, from country to pop to bluegrass to gospel. She is one of six women to have received the Country Music Association award for entertainer of the year. On the heels of two successful TV movies, a series tracing her childhood is reportedly in development.

After more than fifty years in the business, Parton's forty-third solo album, *Pure and Simple*, debuted at number one on the *Billboard* country-album chart in August 2016—her first time in that spot in a quarter century.

Meanwhile, her music has gotten almost no radio play since the early nineties, when Nashville's sound made a dramatic shift away from twang. That didn't keep her fans from packing arenas during her biggest North American tour in twenty-five years, in more than sixty cities.

When I surprised my grandma Betty with tickets to see that tour in Kansas City last summer, at age seventy-one— she and Parton were born eight months apart—she had never before been to a big-arena concert. We are not, as noted, a family with money lying around for tickets to big shows. I had envisioned us wearing matching shirts and emptying a can of Aqua Net onto matching beehives for the occasion, but the trip and all it represented to us—for one thing, I guess, that we weren't as poor as we used to be—was overwhelming enough.

Aside from being the same age, Betty and Dolly share somewhat similar origins. They both had an outhouse at home—Betty's temporary, but an extreme class marker for her generation all the same. They both hated school and felt like outcasts there. Punk before punk was cool, Betty dyed her hair green on St. Patrick's Day when she was a fourteen-year-old waitress in Wichita; when the scandalized boss told her to go home, she refused to return rather than rinse the color out of her hair. As a young woman in the 1960s and 1970s, Betty was a very hot number in big, blond wigs and miniskirts.

Betty fared a little better than Dolly with resources; her family had a car and a small house instead of a cabin, and there were four kids rather than twelve. She drew a far worse hand than Dolly in the parents department, though. Her dad, a factory worker raised on a farm west of Wichita, was a violent alcoholic; her mom, a restaurant cook and sometime factory worker, suffered from untreated mental illness. That might be why Betty went on to live firsthand the life that Dolly apparently only observed and documented in song: the teenage pregnancy, the single motherhood, the violent husbands, the adult poverty.

When I was a kid, Betty would put one of Dolly's tapes in the deck of her old car while we rolled down some highway. It's the only music I remember her singing and crying to in that emotionally repressed Midwestern culture and class.

Watching the concert in Kansas City with Grandma Betty, whose farmhouse I moved into permanently when I was eleven years old and who was just thirty-four when she learned she'd be my grandmother, was like watching two women's lives with roughly similar beginnings but very different outcomes occupy the same space. I found myself watching Betty's reactions more than experiencing my own—a habit anyone from a challenging home might share, as observation becomes a means of both distancing oneself in difficult moments and keeping an eye out for trouble. (People often ask me how, as a writer, I remember so much about my childhood, and I suspect Parton's answer might be the same—if I was going to have a different sort of life, I had to pay close attention to the decisions and situations of those around me.)

Mostly during the concert, though, I was laughing.

"People ask me what it was like to work with Burt Reynolds," Parton said, her tone hinting that it would make a lot more sense to ask Reynolds what it was like to work with her. "Well, my best movie experiences were with women." At the mention of *Steel Magnolias* and *9 to 5*, the crowd thundered happily.

After the last note of her new song "Outside Your Door," in which a horny woman knocks someplace she apparently shouldn't be visiting, Parton said as an afterthought, "Open the dang door. You know you want it." The crowd laughed and cheered.

During a silence a man screamed, "I LOVE YOU DOLLYYYYYY."

"I thought I told you to wait in the truck," she shot back. Even though she's used that line at every show since the Lyndon B. Johnson administration, the crowd laughed and cheered.

She fired her drummer for getting lippy, she explained, but that was OK because the keyboard had a drum machine on it, and it saved her thousands of dollars. The crowd laughed and cheered again.

"Jolene mighta worked at a bank," she said before starting in on that classic, "but I been to the bank many times with this here little song I wrote." The crowd laughed and visibly shook with particular fervor on that one.

Along the way, Betty laughed, too, but not the way she used to. Unlike Parton, she hasn't had high-priced doctors keeping her well-oiled over the years, and her knees were aching in our cramped seats halfway up the enormous arena.

I got her to stand up and dance with me during "9 to 5," for which the whole place was on its feet near the end of the show, but a woman who lived the song might not feel so jubilant.

In the 1970s, Betty got on as a secretary at the county

courthouse in downtown Wichita, did a stint as one of the first female officers in the city's police reserves, and worked her way up to positions as a bailiff, subpoena officer, and probation officer for the criminal courts. She did it all as a woman who attracted a lot of attention from men— including, in that work environment, the same male attorneys who theoretically would represent her in a sexual harassment lawsuit. It can't have been easy.

I was so worried about whether Betty was enjoying herself, if only for knowing she was jonesing for a cigarette, that it took me a while to register that the concert was a pretty big deal for me, too. Though I grew up to be a live-music aficionado, following alt-country acts fervently and helping my then-husband, a professional guitar player, load in and out of bars for years, I had only been to one other mega-concert in my lifetime. That was almost thirty years prior, in the late 1980s, when my dad—a carpenter for whom such a show was also a rare deal—surprised me by taking me to see my favorite singer, Reba McEntire, play the Kansas State Fair.

Before we left our dirt road and took the flat highway to the fairgrounds, Dad recently told me with some regret, he probably drank a couple beers and a whiskey. When we got there, McEntire was just a glittering, sequined speck from where we sat in the bleachers. But it was such a momentous occasion for us that Dad took pictures of the stage with our

110-mm film camera to prove we'd been there while I sang along with every song.

After the concert, merchandise peddlers were out of kids' shirts, if they'd ever had any. So Dad stood in line to buy me all they had left—what was surely a wildly overpriced pink adult-sized T-shirt with a broken heart on it and the name of one of McEntire's big singles at the time, "What Am I Gonna Do About You."

Late at night, when we emerged into the crowded parking lot, Dad's car wouldn't start. Headlights streamed past us until he got the engine going with a stranger's help. I used my huge new T-shirt as a blanket while I slept next to Dad on the long ride home through the dark country, and I wore it as a nightgown for the next two years.

The most poignant thing about that memory, for me, is that my dad—a country boy, the youngest of six kids raised on a farm just down the road from the house he built us with his own hands, money for materials saved from a small concrete-pouring business he ran for a few years—never liked country music and went to the show for his daughter.

"How do you listen to that stuff?" he used to say when my clock radio played 1980s pop-country first thing in the morning and I still needed to be prodded out of bed to catch the school bus. "It's so sad."

In my family, country music was foremost a language

among women. It's how we talked to each other in a place where feelings weren't discussed.

"Listen to the words," Mom used to say, and the song on her record player, eight-track, or tape deck would convey some message about life, about men, about surviving. The voices belonged to Wynonna and Naomi Judd, K. T. Oslin, Janie Fricke, Lorrie Morgan, Anne Murray, and of course to Dolly, Tammy, Patsy, and Loretta. But the information passed from my mother to me, because she was connecting to those songs herself and I was there to hear them. I recall Reba's hit "Little Rock"—not about a town in Arkansas but about slipping a ring off one's finger—being on heavy rotation in our living room not long before my mom divorced my dad.

That I can map my upbringing against a soundtrack of declarative statements sung by women in denim and big hair is one of my greatest blessings. We weren't a family of musicians, but the two women who raised me, my mom and grandma, cared a great deal about music that validated the stories of our lives—working-class girls, women, wives, mothers—in a way that TV shows, movies, books, magazines, and newspapers almost never did.

In the 1980s, when small prairie towns around us were dwindling with economic blight, living in the country meant frequent drives "to town" to buy this or that item or, say, to work at the Wichita mall over the holidays as my mom sometimes did for extra cash. That made for a lot of highway time. Instead of talking to each other, Mom and I both faced forward and sang the same words in unison—country music, usually by women, filling the spaces of silence rolling along flat Kansas landscapes. Mom's cigarette smoke streamed out her cracked window while she held the steering wheel and tapped the air with one of her long, red fingernails.

One song we wore out on a tape together happens to be about women indirectly communicating with each other: "Letter Home," by the Forester Sisters, from their 1988 album *Sincerely*. The lyrics are in the voice of a twenty-nine-year-old woman writing to tell her mom that her husband has run off with someone else and the marriage is over. The year after that single was released, my mom became the newly divorced young woman, albeit for different reasons.

One day when I was grown and sitting in my mother's living room, "Letter Home" came on. We were delighted to find we both remembered all the words. At that moment, I myself was the recently divorced young woman.

Mom went quiet and listened at this verse in particular, like she was hearing it in a new way—now as the mother: "He said he felt like a man with her, and I watched them drive away / Children and rent—there was no time for tears, just time to carry on."

Suddenly incredulous, Mom spoke. "He 'felt like a man with her, and I watched them drive away'?" she said. "How do you feel with this boot up your ass?"

We laughed so hard we doubled over. Neither of us needed to point out that every woman we knew, ourselves included, had only ever done the leaving, not the being left.

Mom stopped laughing at the next verse, though, about the women the narrator works with. One line struck her: "We raise our kids and our jeans still fit / and sometimes we go out at night."

"Our jeans still fit," Mom said quietly and stared into the distance. "Yep." She slowly nodded, her smile gone and one eyebrow lifted in knowing.

What she knew was that the shape of a working-class woman's body has a lot to do with her survival. Not so much because she wants to "catch a man"—the men she has occasion to meet are broke, too, and don't think she doesn't know it—but because the significance of the female form as an object in society is one of the few powers she possesses. Unlike expensive college degrees and high-status material possessions, her body is hers, and how it looks will affect the economic course of her life: Whether she looks nice enough to get the job at the makeup counter. Whether the UPS manager, frowning that she's too small to do the work, can be convinced with a smile in the interview. Whether the banker will approve the shaky loan.

(As it happens, the Forester Sisters' 1991 single "Men," which humorously paints a grim picture of the male gender, has been ironically used by Rush Limbaugh to set up his talk show's recurring "feminist update," which often derides women for their appearance.)

The physical stakes for the working-class woman go beyond those sexual undertones, even, to a matter of simple respect. Poor women are lampooned in popular culture as overweight, having bad teeth, bad clothes. All those signifiers of health and appearance—which are signifiers of class—affect every interaction in a woman's day. For the woman with no money in the bank, each of those interactions decides her and her family's survival.

One woman who understands that, of course, is Dolly Parton.

Parton's musical genius deserves a discussion far beyond and above the matters of gender and class. But the lyrics she wrote are forever tied to the body that sang them, her success forever tied to having patterned her look after the "town trollop" of her native holler. For doing so, she received a fame laced with ridicule; during interviews in the 1970s and 1980s, both Barbara Walters and Oprah Winfrey asked her to stand up so they could point out, without humor, that she looked like a tramp.

Johnny Cash famously wore black as a statement of

rebellion against the status quo and on behalf of the downtrodden and was lauded for it. But that's the difference
between being a man and a woman making a thoughtful
statement with their clothes.

The women who most deeply understand what Parton has
been up to for half a century are the ones who don't have a
voice, a platform, or a college education to articulate it. This,
too, is a source of affection between Parton and some factions
of her audience, perhaps—a secret that hundreds, maybe
thousands, of interviews have not revealed, because writers
and critics don't conceive the question: What role has Dolly
Parton's music, movie roles, and persona played in the lives of
economically disenfranchised women used to being shamed
or cast as victims?

That question has a lot of correct answers, but one of
them is this: At age seventy, Dolly Parton produced a Christmas movie in which a shooed-away sex worker returns at the
end to help a little girl, and she cast herself to play the role.

It's widely discussed that Parton never forgot her roots,
never left behind her community—the economy of which
now revolves around her tourist attractions, the children of
which receive books and scholarships her foundation pro-
vides, the recently incinerated homes of which will be rebuilt
with her help. Less has been said about the extent to which
she never left behind a certain archetype of American woman,

the one whose trailer leads the world to deem her "trash." She isn't necessarily white, but she is necessarily poor, and she most definitely didn't get to study feminist theory in a college classroom.

Parton could've classed herself up decades ago, wearing less makeup as women who can afford it are given to doing, or singing something that doesn't belong on the CD rack at Cracker Barrel. Instead she built her image and wrote her songs so that she can't sing or look in the mirror without representing women who go unheard and unvalidated every day. The conversation between Parton and those women is in the music. They're somewhere wiping down mirrors in truck-stop diner restrooms, listening to country songs while they work.

THE GREAT UNIFIER

One evening last June, before Grandma Betty and I saw Parton on tour, I was scrolling through Twitter, and Parton kept appearing in my feed. It was two days after the United Kingdom voted to withdraw from the European Union, sending cultural and economic shockwaves around the globe. One *New York Times* headline read "Is 'Brexit' the Precursor to a Donald Trump Presidency?" (The column answered the question incorrectly, by the way.) A couple weeks prior, a gunman had killed forty-nine people in a gay nightclub in

Orlando, Florida. In Washington, DC, Democrats had just stormed the House floor to stage a sit-in for passage of gun-control legislation.

But, amid the dark political tweet-cloud on my computer screen, Parton appeared, holding a tiny bedazzled saxophone. A couple tweets down, here she was again, this time in a video singing 1960s protest songs a cappella with her small band. Political tweet, political tweet—then Parton again! I realized that several of my friends in New York City were at her show in Queens.

She'd recently kicked off the Pure and Simple tour, which I hadn't even known was going on. I was confused—what were a bunch of New Yorkers doing knowing more about Dolly than I did?

The Dolly tweets piping in from New York contacts were from a group that crossed lines of race, ethnicity, religion, and sexual orientation. They were all, however, women.

"That majestic bitch just started playing a goddamn PANFLUTE [sic]," one tweeted.

"Dolly Parton, sitting in a pew onstage, just got a stadium full of Nyers to shout 'Amen,'" said another. And then: "Nothing says #Pride like a stadium full of gays singing 'Here You Come Again' with Dolly Parton."

Suddenly two New York acquaintances I didn't realize knew one another were tweeting an exchange.

"Her voice is perfect."

"Dolly forever! Who knew she was such a storyteller?"

"About to fling myself at the stage."

At that moment, not yet having been among Parton's live audiences, I was amused, touched, and a little surprised. I've been chided about country music so many times that, when I lived for a couple years in New York, I hosted a party with the sole purpose of teaching people how to line dance and sending them home with CD mixes of something other than hipster-approved David Allen Coe. I guess I figured that Dolly Parton would only be loved ironically in some places.

I knew Parton was an icon beloved around the world, of course, but I hadn't realized the extent to which people who aren't "country" appreciate her—not just as a "crossover" artist but as the down-home, even religious persona she embodied in that recent tour. Perhaps the most remarkable thing about her steadfast focus on tales of poverty and rural life, sung from beneath a wig and rhinestones, is how much she is universally adored for it by people whose backgrounds couldn't be more different from hers.

My connection to Parton and her music as a fellow working-class woman from the country is just one facet of her appeal. Plenty of stars enjoy massive audiences, but Parton's work and persona create a connection among seemingly unlikely friends.

Amid the crowds for last year's tour, Dolly drag queens turned and directed entire sections to sway with the beat. Those who swayed appeared to include wrinkled people wearing Wrangler jeans, pierced teenagers wearing all black, big men wearing T-shirts that read "proud redneck," gay men who knew the words to every song, children who knew the same words, lesbian couples holding hands, college kids holding a beer in both hands, seen-it-all women like my grandma Betty, and most everything in between.

Being among them, one sees and feels the power of a woman who truly lives the teachings of Jesus—love all, judge not—in contrast to the hollow Christianity so much of Nashville's country music machine falsely espouses. It is an energy that cannot be faked. Everyone there feels it, and Parton directly acknowledges it.

"Wouldn't it be nice if we could take a little vial of this love energy out there?" she asked the Austin crowd last December. People clapped and cried at the end of a very hard year in America, on the cusp of what was sure to be another hard one.

Parton almost always eschews politics, but she caught hell from both sides of the partisan divide last year for her approach to the presidential election. When the *New York Times* asked her what she thought about a woman running for president, Parton responded enthusiastically.

"Hillary [Clinton] might make as good a president as anybody ever has," she said. ". . . I personally think a woman would do a great job. I think Hillary's very qualified. So if she gets it, I'll certainly be behind her."

Part of her conservative fan base shrieked in the blogosphere and social media, swearing they'd never buy her records or concert tickets again. Parton followed up with a statement to say that "if she gets it" referred to the presidency, not to the Democratic nomination, which wasn't yet official.

"My comment about supporting a woman in the White House was taken out of context," the statement read. She hadn't endorsed either candidate, she said, in future interviews taking the line that she hadn't even decided yet.

The left, then, shrieked at the idea that she would even consider a vote for Donald Trump, who by then was the Republican nominee. They, too, would never buy her records or concert tickets again.

The vast majority will probably keep on buying, of course. Parton is a great unifier not just across differences in identity and background but also across today's devastating political chasm.

On her 2016 concert tour, Parton wove in her signature puns and self-deprecating jokes: Whether Clinton or Trump got in, the country would suffer from "PMS" either way—

"presidential mood swings." She doesn't like to get political, but if she did run, she had the hair for it—it's huuuuuge, she said, imitating Trump. But then again maybe they didn't need any more "boobs" in the race.

Such crowd-pleasing diplomacy might have something to do with business, but Parton has put her sales on the line many times in the same political climate that saw the Dixie Chicks ostracized by Nashville and country radio when they denounced then-president George W. Bush after the 2003 invasion of Iraq.

In 2006, for example, after decades of vocal support for the LGBTQ community, she wrote a song for the *Transamerica* soundtrack, "Travelin' Thru." The song, which she performed at the Academy Awards when it was a best-song nominee, alludes to roots music about hard, transformative journeys, including the nineteenth-century folk song "Wayfaring Stranger" and the early twentieth-century country gospel song "I Am a Pilgrim." The soundtrack number weaves that history in as it honors the personal, public, and political struggles of people transitioning genders. Parton sings in their voice, "We've all been crucified, and they nailed Jesus to the tree / And when I'm born again, you're gonna see a change in me."

Parton reportedly received death threats for participating in the movie. But she empathizes with those vilified or considered "freaks" for their experience of sexuality or gender, she has said, as a cisgender, straight woman whose appearance is considered abnormal and whose sex life has been prodded. Rumors have flown for years about a lesbian relationship with a childhood friend who is often at her side. She insists she would proudly come out if that were the case; she has been married to the same man, a Tennessean who worked in the concrete business, for fifty years. What her LGBTQ fans respond to, she says, is not her own sexuality but her non-judgmental embrace of theirs.

Parton's aversion to overt political discourse might have a lot to do with where she's from. Many members of my family don't like talking about politics either—not because they don't care, but because they don't have the trained language or time required to engage with the chattering class.

I am a professional communicator with three college degrees, and even I have been shamed for using the wrong word or framework on Twitter. My view wasn't systemic enough, or my term wasn't the most frequent currency in intellectual jargon. Imagine if, like Parton and the women in my family, you hadn't been in school since you were a teenager in a rural area before the internet existed. I don't care how worldly you get; if that's your background, conversation dominated by formal, academic voices likely will feel intimidating or at least uncomfortable. See Parton's 2009 commencement speech at the University of Tennessee in which she admits that, for all the stages she has commanded, she is nervous speaking before an auditorium full of people in caps and gowns. Her voice shakes while she says it—a startling thing to watch in a woman whose profound confidence has publicly shone forth for decades.

Whatever Parton's reasons for conveying personal stories rather than polemics, that proclivity couldn't come at a better time in a world reeling with discord. Several of my friends—white, Black, and Latina, with disparate class origins among them—commented in the weeks surrounding the 2016 presidential election that Parton was a balm of sorts, a spiritual leader when political leaders are failing.

Like any transcendent storyteller, her politics occur at the human level, examined as experience rather than abstract concepts and lived directly rather than bandied in academic terms. There is an important place for both the story that speaks for itself and the didactic argument. Parton deals in the former.

Last year she made a statement about race and immigration, not with a political tweet but through her philanthropy's commitment to reach every victim of the Tennessee wildfires. According to Dollywood Foundation executive director Jeff Conyers, the organization was concerned that immigrants without legal status would forgo applying for help. The foundation thus reached out to leaders in the Hispanic community to convey across language barriers that they weren't "out to catch" anyone. No questions were asked or records kept about race, ethnicity, or citizenship in connecting people with relief funds. In a similar vein, no reports or follow-ups were required from recipients, and they were trusted to spend the assistance money however they wished.

I think again of my West Virginia friend's comment after those wildfires: "Dolly will save 'em."

One reason she can do so, it seems, is that a lifetime of projecting love while staying off doctrine inspires good acts in others. Last December, she and her foundation put on an old-fashioned telethon, also livestreamed online, to raise money for the fire victims. In a matter of hours they racked up $9 million. Performers who showed up when Parton called ranged from pop legend Cyndi Lauper to new country star Chris Stapleton. Paul Simon called in with a $100,000 pledge while Parton was talking with Billy Ray Cyrus.

Parton has friends in many places. As I was typing this story in a Wichita coffee shop, a man who said he was homeless asked me what I was writing about. When I told him, he lit up and regaled me with Parton's life story, ending on a note of admiration for the integrity of her voice in an era of digitally manipulated music.

"She don't need none of that," he said. "No matter how many years pass and no matter what she looks like, her pipes are her pipes."

Maybe it's no coincidence that Parton's popularity seemed to surge the same year America seemed to falter. A fractured thing craves wholeness, and that's what Dolly Parton offers—one woman who simultaneously embodies past and present, rich and poor, feminine and masculine, Jezebel and Holy Mother, the journey of getting out and the sweet return to home.

To quote one of my New York City acquaintances live-tweeting from Parton's show last June, "This is just everything."

THE LAST LAUGH

Parton jokes that she had to get rich to sing like she was poor again.

Down in that holler in the middle of the twentieth century, she was the same spirit inside a gifted poor girl. She had a loving family, a guitar, and an uncle for a mentor, and she longed to get gone to wherever she would be seen. Parton was the target of cruel gossip in high school, she has said—rumors about what sort of girl she was. She couldn't leave before she turned eighteen, she has said, because she figured her daddy would send a posse after her.

When she graduated from Sevier County High in 1964— the first person from her family to earn a diploma—each member of the class was asked to stand up and share their plans. As she would recount in her University of Tennessee commencement address, she told her classmates she was going to Nashville to become a star. They burst out in laughter.

The next day, she hugged her family goodbye and went to the bus station.

While waiting for the bus, her life was on the cusp of great change, and so was the world. Within weeks, the Civil Rights Act would be signed into law. The biggest women's movement since the fight for suffrage was brewing. But Parton's experience in East Tennessee would be the foundation for her songwriting, a guidebook for carefully handling Nashville's men in suits, and a summons to share wealth with people who need it.

Parton didn't know all that. All she knew was that she was moving to a big, new place to do something she'd already been working toward for years. She carried everything she owned in her hands. Somewhere deeper, she carried a belief that she was worth more than the world had suggested and an abiding humor about what she had endured along the way.

"I boarded a Greyhound bus with my dreams, my old guitar, the songs I had written," she said in her autobiography, setting up a joke she has told many times, "and the rest of my belongings in a set of matching luggage—three paper bags from the same grocery store."

PART TWO

DOLLY PARTON MASTERS
THE ART OF LEAVING

PART TWO

DOLLY PARTON MASTERS
THE ART OF LEAVING

In 2014, *Billboard* magazine asked Dolly Parton about feminism. "Are you familiar with Sheryl Sandberg's book *Lean In*?" the interviewer inquired.

"What is it?" Parton asked.

"*Lean In*—it is a book," the interviewer explained. "Have you ever 'leaned in'?"

"I've leaned over," Parton said, cracking herself up with a possible innuendo. "I've leaned forward. I don't know what 'leaned in' is."

That an iconic female trailblazer in music, business, and popular culture wasn't up on the feminist conversation du jour might reveal Parton's origins: a place where a woman's strength and independence are more about walk than talk. In the women's movement, that talk—the articulation, study, and theories of advancement toward gender parity—has been crucial to social progress. Of equal import and less acclaim, though, is what poor and working-class women do for the cause.

Their worlds often resist the container of politicized terminology, which is usually the province of college-educated people. But "uneducated" women have seen the most devastating outcomes of gender inequality: impoverished mothers with hungry children, abused wives too poor and rural to access the legal system, work that is not only undervalued and underpaid but makes the fingers bleed. For these women, the fight to merely survive is a declaration of equality that could be called "feminist." But here's the thing: In my experience, right or wrong, they don't give a shit what you call it.

Earlier this year, the Women's March and related strike on International Women's Day again exposed the old class chasm that tends to run through any political movement. With the Oval Office newly occupied by an admitted sexual predator, today's crucial political resistance owes much to the hard work and fury of civically engaged women. Who is able to participate in such activism has a lot to do with economic agency, though. You can bet that most photos of marchers wearing pink "pussy" hats document middle- or upper-class women able to take time away from work, obtain transportation to a protest site, or afford a babysitter.

For a woman like me, a feminist who grew up in a place that was more like Dolly Parton's childhood home in rural Tennessee than like a well-connected progressive hub, marches and strikes are something to simultaneously cheer and look upon with some skepticism. I'm proud to call myself a feminist but feel no self-satisfaction about my framework for the term—a privilege of education and culture most women where I'm from have not experienced.

Working-class women might not be fighting for a cause with words, time, and money they don't have, but they possess an unsurpassed wisdom about the way gender works in the world. Take, for example, the concept of intersectionality. A working-class woman of color might not know that word, but she knows better than anyone how her race, gender, and economic struggles intertwine.

There is, then, intellectual knowledge—the stuff of research studies and think pieces—and there is experiential knowing. Both are important, and women from all backgrounds might possess both. But we rarely exalt the knowing, which is the only kind of feminism many working women have.

LEAVING HOME

Parton's career took off at the same moment the women's liberation movement did, providing a revealing contrast between feminism as political concept and feminism embodied in the world. Like most women in poverty, Parton knew little of the former but excelled at the latter.

You won't get very far as a poor woman without believing you are equal to men. The result of that belief is unlikely to be a "leaning in," Sandberg's possibly sound advice to middle- and upper-class women seeking to claim the spoils enjoyed by the men in their offices and homes. A poor woman's better solution is often to turn around and walk away from a hopelessly patriarchal situation that she cannot possibly mend with her limited cultural capital.

When Parton left Sevier County, Tennessee, it was 1964, a presidential election year, and the country was torn by political uprising and tragedy. Young men were returning from Vietnam in caskets, and President John F. Kennedy had been assassinated less than a year prior.

In her 1994 autobiography, *Dolly: My Life and Other Unfinished Business*, Parton recalled hearing news of Kennedy's death over her boyfriend's car radio while en route to perform on the Cas Walker radio show during a school break.

"I had loved John Kennedy . . . in the way one idealist recognizes another and loves him for that place within themselves that they share," she wrote. "I didn't know a lot about politics, but I knew that a lot of things were wrong and unjust and that Kennedy wanted to change them." Her boyfriend, however, responded to the announcement by calling Kennedy a "nigger-lovin' son of a bitch." She promptly dumped him.

"I couldn't believe that young person with whom I had shared intimacy and laughter could be so ignorant, biased, and insensitive," she recalled.

The women's liberation movement of the 1960s and 1970s had not yet reached fever pitch. Kennedy had created a commission on the status of women, but the National Organization for Women did not yet exist. Strict, conformist gender roles still trapped females of all socioeconomic classes as wives, mothers, and second-class citizens.

When Parton stepped off the bus in Nashville, some of that movement's foundational texts were yet to be published, but they likely wouldn't have reached Parton anyhow. The women of her lot were too busy feeding hungry mouths, some further isolated from discourse in a pre-internet, rural place, to read such literature—written in a form of English they didn't speak, anyway. That Parton even learned to read was a privilege that her father, a farmer and sometimes coal miner who was illiterate for lack of schooling, didn't share.

But Parton was living feminism without reading about it. Leaving home alone, as a woman with professional aspirations and no financial means, demonstrated that she wanted a better life and thought she deserved it, though no model existed for the journey ahead beyond her own imagination.

Meanwhile, the place where she'd pursue that life—the recording capital of country music—couldn't have been a more harrowing gantlet for a woman. Even if America had by then put a few small cracks in the ceiling that held women down, Nashville was squarely situated under the thickest glass.

Patsy Cline, who died in a plane crash the year before Parton got to town, had recently challenged the industry's old-boy network, in which women almost never headlined shows. In 1960, she dared to wear pants onstage at the Grand Ole Opry and was called over by a male host to be reprimanded before the crowd. That was the sort of heat headstrong Cline was born to take and dish back, but she couldn't beat economic injustice as she trailblazed for her gender. According to the PBS documentary *American Masters: Patsy Cline*, her first record deal, in the 1950s, gave her half the industry-standard pay rate men received and reserved all publishing rights for her label. This enslaved her voice to the studio's demands. But Cline—eager to escape her own poor, working-class origins in Virginia—found it preferable to her previous job slitting chicken throats on an assembly line.

It was a hard row for a female singer-songwriter, and Parton's dreams didn't materialize as quickly as she'd hoped. She was soon so broke she fed herself by stealing food from grocery stores or roaming hotel hallways in search of room-service trays left outside doors for pickup.

Over the course of a few years, she made a small name for

herself around town doing mercenary gigs: live spots on early-morning radio shows, a jukebox convention in Chicago. She garnered attention as the uncredited backup singer on a hit pop song she had cowritten with her uncle, "Put It Off Until Tomorrow," which was named BMI Song of the Year. The next year, 1967, Parton finally got the chance to cut her first country song, "Dumb Blonde." It became a Top 10 hit.

The irony of a song called "Dumb Blonde"—an admonishment of a man who calls a woman stupid—being Parton's big break is supreme. Its theme, a woman being smarter than the man who underestimates her, would be a recurring one throughout her career. Parton didn't write that song, as she would most of her hits to come, but she lived it so thoroughly that she couldn't even perform it on television without a man doing the precise thing the song articulates.

To perform her popular number on the syndicated *The Bobby Lord Show*, twenty-one-year-old Parton wore a fitted orange dress with a high neckline. Her massive blond beehive may have reached a couple inches higher than the mainstream norm, but there was no obvious trace of country or the over-the-top look for which she's now known.

When Parton spoke, though, her East Tennessee accent showed, as did the fact that she was more capable than the male host. Someone had written a goofy segue to her performance in which Lord apparently was supposed to cleverly call her a dumb blonde with a well-timed pause—as in, "Why don't you go sing, dumb blonde," rather than, "Why don't you go sing 'Dumb Blonde.'" Parton did her part—act confused and smile—but even on the second try Lord couldn't deliver the line right, and the joke flopped.

Still, suffering those sorts of indignities for exposure or a small check turned out to be a good gamble. Porter Wagoner, whose country music hour was the number-one nationally syndicated show on television, said he'd been following Parton's work and saw "something magical" in her, she recalled in her autobiography. Would she join his show? The salary offer: sixty grand.

It was a rip-off considering Wagoner and the show's wealth, but it was a fortune in Parton's eyes. She said yes, of course.

Parton's big risk—leaving home as a teenager without two dimes to rub together at an age by which her own mother was already married with two children in a Smoky Mountain holler—had paid off. She had ended up in another sort of bind, though: what would turn out to be a long, often torturous tenure alongside the male host's thunderous ego on *The Porter Wagoner Show*. But Parton would never haunt hotel hallways seeking scraps of room-service meals again.

With that first bit of money, according to the 2014 interview with *Billboard*, Parton bought her first new car. She was married by then, to a man who ran a concrete-pouring business, and his preferences decided what kind of car it would be.

"I think it was a Chevrolet," Parton said, "because Carl, at that time, only drove Chevrolets."

Like many women then and certainly poor ones, she didn't know how to drive. En route to record with Wagoner for the first time, she drove the blue station wagon into the wall of Nashville's Studio A. That she rolled up and knocked bricks off a powerful recording studio in the man's world where she was tearing down walls has some poetic significance. The bricks were replaced but never quite matched.

"When [the studio] used to do tours," she told *Billboard*, "they'd go around and say, 'This is where Dolly Parton ran into the wall.'"

HAVING ENOUGH

Most poor women's risks don't pay off with fame and fortune. But the lives of the women I grew up around—airplane-factory workers, cafeteria cooks, discount-store cashiers, diner waitresses, fast-food workers—all contain a common thread of dramatic, self-preserving departures. The stories they told me about their pasts and presents could be boiled down to a recurring line: "I had enough of his shit."

The "he" in the story might be an abusive husband, a cheating boyfriend, a mean boss. Sometimes it was a place rather than a man that was hostile—the small Colorado town that ostracized my then-twenty-something grandmother for wearing mini-skirts and not behaving "properly" in the 1960s, or the Kansas community where her teenage sister was shamed for being pregnant out of wedlock. For them, the act of leaving wasn't so much hopeful as it was necessary for survival, whether physically or psychologically. Often, my family's circumstances being what they were, the next man or place was no better than the last. But they could leave again, and they did. By the time she was thirty-two, my grandma Betty had divorced six men.

The first one shot her. The second one kidnapped her son. The third one broke her jaw. The fourth one was a brief business arrangement: She could show the courts she had a husband, as an attorney had insisted amid her attempts to get her son back, and he, a Mexican immigrant, could get his US visa. The fifth turned out to be irrevocably emotionally scarred from his time serving in Vietnam. The sixth one was verbally critical of Betty and my mom, who by then was a teenager.

As my grandma would say about any intolerable situation she left behind, "It wasn't gonna get it."

Most of that relationship drifting occurred prior to the height of second-wave feminism, about which Betty knew nothing. She didn't know the patriarchal history of the institution of marriage, which middle-class females of coming decades would learn in women's studies classes and discuss at meetings. She had never encountered the term "patriarchy" (nor had I until I was a young woman in college). She only knew that she wouldn't let a man, town, or boss mistreat her or her children.

Over those years, jobs and locations proved just as impermanent as romance. Betty worked countless gigs and drove all over the country with my mother, great-grandmother, and aunts in search of a better place, smoke streaming out of a rattling jalopy's window, a cigarette in the hand that no longer wore a ring.

One might be tempted to speculate that a woman with that sort of résumé can't stay put, that it's her nature rather than her circumstances that causes her to find trouble and leave again and again. Maybe even that a lack of self-respect drew her to horrible situations. But that would be underestimating the number of hard hands a young woman in poverty in the 1960s could be dealt in a row.

When Betty finally got dealt a couple good hands, she held onto her cards. Around age thirty, when a job-training grant for women helped her land a position as a secretary in the Kansas courts system in downtown Wichita, she became a state employee and remained one for decades until her retirement. Soon after that, when she met the man I grew up knowing as my grandfather—a fun, kind farmer and the first man in her life who had ever treated her right—she married him and lived on his farm for the next twenty-two years, until his death.

A woman of middle-class means might fight for parity with men in her corporate office and insist that her husband change diapers and vacuum; she might organize political meetings and write letters to local newspaper editors demanding her daughter's basketball team receive coverage on par with her son's; she might donate money to Planned Parenthood and use some of her hard-earned savings to spend a weekend marching with fellow women in the nation's capital. All these admirable actions involve leveraging some existing sliver of agency within an institution to change it. That middle-class woman is working to improve a woman's place inside the workforce, domestic life, public policy, politics. Those realms have become hospitable enough for her that she might stick around and alter them.

For the poor woman, there is much less social, economic, or cultural capital for changing a situation from the inside. But she might have a car and a bit of money for gas, which is enough to leave a situation behind.

Regardless of one's economic lot, there's a powerful wisdom in just leaving the bullshit for someone else to fix. I knew this when I was a professor at a small university with a curious history of tenured female professors resigning. Sometimes even middle-class women, those of us who could stay and try to change the worlds in which we find ourselves, realize we could give our entire lives to shift things an inch. Is the inch worth our lives? I resigned five months after I was tenured.

Several of my middle-class female friends worried I'd lost my mind. At the time, I had no financial security or prospects outside that job. I did have a mortgage and a load of student debt. But my job at that university, I found, involved a daily grind of sexism not so different in essence from the slaps on the ass I'd gotten for seven years as a waitress. Ultimately, it wasn't gonna get it. Two women who asked no questions, only quietly nodded yes with a deep knowing, were my mom and Grandma Betty.

In that moment, I left the broader institution of universities and college campuses that I'd harnessed to climb out of poverty. After a few immediate years back in the poor house, it turned out to be a very good decision—perhaps the boldest feminist act I will ever make, and one through which dreams came true. I owe the boldness that I tapped to the poor women in my blood. Sometimes a woman who knows her worth ought to lean in. But sometimes she ought to just leave.

The tension between those two strategies is one Parton would come to know well as Porter Wagoner's young female co-star on a show that bore his name.

Wagoner, who had a string of country hits in the 1950s, was a cunning business force who had leveraged the new television medium before most music artists knew what to do with it. Born in a small town in the Ozarks of southern Missouri, he was a self-made man with an ego that outshone his rhinestone-bedazzled Nudie Cohn suits. He was an imposing physical presence—tall with a long face, yellow pompadour, and serious demeanor. By contrast, Dolly was five feet tall, wearing demure dresses and a bright, genuine smile. Parton would become known for flashy looks later in her career, but on Wagoner's show it's clear that he was the one more precious about his appearance.

Wagoner was old enough to be her father, but Parton had been hired as the variety-show equivalent of a romantic lead. She was meant to be the pretty thing at his side, singing duets in which man and woman play lovers. But Wagoner would get more than he bargained for.

Initially skeptical of Parton replacing the former female co-star, Norma Jean, audiences soon cared more about Parton than they did about the host. Both she and Wagoner put out solo records alongside the duets, and hers outsold his. They both wrote songs, and hers were better.

The more threatened Wagoner felt, according to Parton's autobiography, the more tightly he tried to control Parton and her career—telling her what she should sing, what she should write, whether she was allowed to write, who would publish the songs. In her autobiography, Parton recalled feeling wary of conflict. Wagoner was a blustery screamer when he didn't get his way, and hers was a quiet strength; he was a tortured soul who needed to be puffed up, and she was a stable, empathetic friend willing to sacrifice and give a lot. Theirs had the makings of a classic abusive relationship.

Straight out of the controlling-male playbook, Wagoner did anything he could to push other male business influences out of her life. He shut out her uncle Billy Owens, who had been her musical mentor and industry advocate for years. He insisted she leave her close friend and producer Fred Foster at Monument Records for RCA, where Wagoner acted as an intermediary on the deal. He wanted her to succeed, yes, and her success helped his. As her star rose, though, he became increasingly competitive and possessive.

During a television interview they did together in 1971, which can now be found online, he hooked his long arm around her small shoulders—a jealous-boyfriend maneuver many women would recognize—and told her when to speak.

They had no romantic relationship, according to Parton, who has never called his actions sexual harassment. But romance rumors inevitably circulate about male and female co-stars. In her autobiography, Parton hinted that Wagoner might have encouraged those rumors. Tammy Wynette occasionally filled in for Parton on the show, and Parton recalled Wynette's concern about Wagoner's power to diminish both of their reputations through his tales of sexual conquest.

"One day I was talking to Tammy and she asked me, 'What if Porter claims we all slept with him?'" Parton wrote. "'Don't worry, Tammy,' I said. 'Half of the people will think he's lying and the other half will just think we have bad taste.'"

Parton might have smiled through Wagoner's power plays, but a close look at their on-screen banter reveals a woman who knows exactly what is happening and will meet every slight with a subtle move capable of dismantling Wagoner's thin veneer of poise.

"You wanna put your guitar away and we'll sing a duet, or you wanna just keep it?" Wagoner asks in one segue into a duet for which he will play guitar. His tone sounds like a command rather than a question.

"I'll just hang on to it," Parton says, as if to say, nah, I'm good, you son of a bitch.

"Okay," Wagoner replies through a forced smile.

"I need a security blanket," Parton adds—seeming self-deprecation that draws a boundary of self-preservation. Then Wagoner lays into the strings and they sing "Her and the Car and the Mobile Home," from their 1972 duet album, *The Right Combination—Burning the Midnight Oil.* The song is about a cheating husband returning home to find his suffering wife has left for good.

During the same episode, while introducing a solo performance by Parton, Wagoner makes a joke she doesn't like. From off-camera, she talks back, joke-arguing with what he's said. For a second, his big smile falls.

"Shut up," he says flatly, and then the big smile returns and Parton sings her enduring classic "Tennessee Mountain Home."

Perhaps it's no coincidence that Wagoner's aggression is on full display in that episode from 1972—the year Parton's five-year contract with him was up.

Wagoner convinced Parton to stay on past her contract terms, but tension between them only increased. In one particularly barbed exchange during a 1973 episode, the awkwardness of which *Rolling Stone* explored in 2016, the sweet girl Wagoner hired is now a fierce woman who is just about done.

"We're back again," Wagoner says, wrapping his arm around Parton's shoulders. "Me and my sidekick here. She just kicked me in the side." Wagoner flinches and gasps to pretend Parton has struck him, and they both smile and laugh.

Parton turns and looks up at his face. "Not yet, but I think I will after that," she says.

Wagoner's arm falls away from her, and his smile falls away from his face—this time for more than just a second.

"Ohhh," he trails. "If you ever hit me and I find it out, Dolly Parton, you'll be in trouble."

Then, within seconds, they are smiling and bobbing through the conversational duet "Run That by Me One More Time," in which a man lies about where he's been and a woman lies about how much money she spent.

At the end of the number, Wagoner summons someone from the audience to join them onstage. It's Jimmy Dean, the country singer—an enormous man who enters the shot as a lumbering blue suit headed for Parton with his arms outstretched. He forces himself onto Parton while she laughs and pushes at him to keep their torsos apart for an uncomfortably long moment. Parton has held her own against Wagoner in a verbal fencing match, only to be physically accosted by a man whose name was synonymous with sausage.

The courage and audacity Parton summoned in those moments might be lost on us today. She had escaped a world of physical labor, but her presence in male-dominated spaces came with few protections. Maybe it's a blessing that she got married soon after arriving in Nashville; while so many men would disrespect a single woman, some would avoid harassing one who wears a wedding band, whether because they see her as being "claimed" or for fear of a whoopin' from her husband.

Wagoner, though, was Parton's husband in the public's eye, and the same spunk that was driving him mad helped him turn a massive profit. In the studio recording of "Run That by Me One More Time," Wagoner says at the end, in his speaking voice, "I ought to box your jaws." Parton responds, "Aw, you'd hit your mama before you hit me."

This humorous bravado in the face of an unfunny threat is a signature of female country music and the culture of working-class women. My grandma Betty, you'll recall, really did have her jaw broken by an angry husband as she was leaving him. She was twenty-three, poor with two kids, and he was soon to be her third ex-husband. She told me about it with a laugh.

"Feel this," she said, jutting her chin toward me and putting my hand on it. I felt her lower jaw, as she shifted it to one side and it made a big click, slightly out of joint as it had been for almost fifty years. "That was a gift from one of my sweethearts."

Like so many women, Betty had lived a life more privileged classes sometimes say is "like a country song"—a backward analysis. Artists like Parton intentionally told the stories of the women they knew, otherwise voiceless in society. In other words, the living came before the song. Parton has never strayed from representing them, whether in the lyrics she wrote or the woman she is. On Wagoner's show, she'd prove to be the woman in "Her and the Car and the Mobile Home," who makes off with the trailer in the end.

ESCAPE ARTISTS

People can be found packing up and leaving in the lyrics of most music genres, but there is something particularly poor, female, and American about the leaving that happens in country music. You could think of the woman in these songs as the counterpart to the rambling male outlaw who sings of gambling, honky-tonks, and trains.

Those men's lyrics often claim a lady is waiting back home, admirably suffering her mate's neglect. The rough-hewn women I know are more like the one in the early nineties Lorrie Morgan hit "Watch Me" (also, as it happens, written by men); she tells a doubtful partner that she really will leave, and you can hear in her voice which one of them is right. In "Wrong Side of Memphis," Trisha Yearwood puts a '69 Tempest on Highway 40 and points it toward Nashville to chase her childhood dream of playing the Opry because she's got nothing to lose. Such departures are made possible by the personal freedoms and geographic expanses of the United States that are more often associated with male adventures.

Leaving pervades the broader world of roots music, too. In her two biggest hits, Tracy Chapman skeptically asks for one good reason to stay and plans to leave a hard life behind with a fast car and some money that she saved working at the convenience store.

The hard-up woman is less tethered to place than the middle-class one, whose more stable, rooted existence involves a good job, a gym membership, and a leadership post in community organizations. The poor woman will have a harder time finding resources for hitting the road, but in spirit she is what they call a flight risk, and what she longs to fly away from is more than just a wayward man. It's a small town, a brutal job, an entire class.

In "Boston Town," bluegrass band Della Mae speaks as one of the women of the famous 1912 Bread and Roses Strike in Lawrence, Massachusetts, where nearly thirty thousand ethnically diverse textile workers, most of them female immigrants, joined forces to expose dangerous work conditions and demand better wages.

"They said what a waste of a pretty girl / to let the labor flag unfurl," the song goes. "I said, what more can you take from me? / I own my hands and my dignity."

"Boston Town" is a rare exaltation of working-class female strength at the root of social change—which is precisely what many of Parton's early songs are about. She just tells them at the ground level, in the hearts and homes of women.

Parton's early songs also document the woman not yet freed, the moment just before progress. These are not tales about cars and horizons but rather dark, minor-key acknowledgments of situations a woman might need to escape. Over and over, young Parton sings about women who are stuck in a place of cultural and economic subjugation.

Parton's first hit with RCA, 1968's "Just Because I'm a Woman," illuminated the sexual double standards that encouraged men to be playboys but morally incriminated the women who slept with them. The song follows a traditional country-guitar strum, but the ideas Parton pushed through Nashville in the lyrics were as revolutionary as the feminist publications coming out of academia and radical small presses.

Responding to a disappointed partner's admonishment, the song describes "slut shaming" long before that was a term: "Yes I've made mistakes, but listen and understand / My mistakes are no worse than yours just because I'm a woman."

Parton goes on to sing of a woman's ruined reputation and her sexual partner leaving her to propose marriage to a virgin "angel."

Parton has said she got the idea for the song from her own

life. She had grown up pushing the boundaries of acceptable behavior in the religious backwoods of Tennessee, she wrote in her autobiography, a place where smudging a burnt matchstick around her lashes as eyeliner was the stuff of scandal.

When she met a handsome man named Carl Dean at a laundry facility in Nashville just after getting to town, he soon decided they were meant to get hitched. He also assumed a woman as nice as Dolly must also be a "nice girl." Eight months after their wedding, he decided to ask if she'd been with other men before him.

"I assumed it didn't matter," she told *Entertainment Weekly* in 2009. ". . . I figured the truth was better, because I didn't want to start a marriage with a lie." The truth crushed him, and he moped around about it for months.

"He could not get over that for the longest time," she told *Rolling Stone* in 2003. "I thought, 'Well, my goodness, what's the big damn deal?' "

To her great satisfaction, the song she got out of that marital conflict, "Just Because I'm a Woman," reached the Top 20 chart in South Africa a few years after its US release. "All those oppressed women!" she exclaimed about it in the *Rolling Stone* profile.

Parton continued to challenge the false saint-or-whore dichotomy with the title track of her 1975 release "The Bargain Store," which Wagoner co-produced with Bob Ferguson at RCA. In the song, a haunting but self-assured plea from a woman to her would-be lover, a woman compares herself to merchandise that has been used and even damaged but is nonetheless still in good-enough condition. The bold chorus might even reference more than just an open heart: "The bargain store is open—come inside."

Parton recalled in the *Entertainment Weekly* interview that "a lot of stations wouldn't play it because they thought it was about a whore." The single nonetheless climbed the charts to be her fifth number-one solo song.

Parton's 1970 album, *The Fairest of Them All*, recorded about halfway through her time on *The Porter Wagoner Show*, is made of Parton originals that bear witness to the horrors endured by women at the physical and economic mercy of men and their desires. The album title references a sexist fairy tale, of course; on the cover, Parton smiles into a mirror with the fresh face of Snow White, but her tall ruff evokes the wicked queen.

In "Daddy Come and Get Me," a grown daughter begs her father to rescue her from a mental institution where her husband has committed her so that he can be with another woman. That song shed light on the centuries-old practice of branding a sane woman "crazy" and institutionalizing her when it suited a man's purpose, still a phenomenon in psychiatry in the 1970s.

On the third track of *Fairest*, a woman tells her lover

that she will leave if he tries to change or control her. "I'll be movin' on when possession gets too strong," Parton sings.

In "I'm Doing This for Your Sake," a woman's heart breaks as she tells a baby she must give it up for adoption since the father ran off; to get her in bed, he promised her they'd get married and then split once he heard she was pregnant.

The songwriting jewel of the album, "Down from Dover," sounds like pop-country in 1970: steel guitar, tambourine, backup vocals, a bit of harpsichord layered against a mid-tempo melody. But it's classic Parton storytelling from that early point in her career, when the ghosts of the women's fates she has escaped are still close at her heels. In the story, a teenage girl gets pregnant and is shamed and kicked out of the house by her parents. The baby's father has left town, giving her a line that he'll be back to marry her before she starts showing. She prays for the boy to return, but seasons change without any word. In autumn, she goes into labor alone and delivers a stillborn daughter without medical help: "I guess in some strange way she knew she'd never have a father's arms to hold her / And dying was her way of telling me he wasn't coming down from Dover."

The song remains one of Parton's favorites, she has said, and was covered by Marianne Faithfull and Nancy Sinatra. Just a few years before she recorded it, she had been smiling and bobbing to "Dumb Blonde"—a song written by a man, conveying some sass but lacking the gravity Parton brought with her from Sevier County's hollers. Now, she was telling gothic stories about women that were too true to even get played on the radio. RCA wouldn't release "Dover" as a single, Parton would recall, due to its controversial theme of pregnancy out of wedlock.

She'd written the song when she was just eighteen, she has told crowds when introducing the number, but she would be in her thirties before society was ready to hear her sing it.

"It was just a story about a girl havin' a baby—nothin' that really unnatural about that," she told a 1983 London audience. "She thought somebody loved her, he left her in trouble, and never came back—but that seemed to be too heavy at the time."

In the 1960s and 1970s, Parton had left home for the lights of Nashville and found success. But, in some ways, she was just as trapped as she would have been as a knocked-up kid in a shack in Sevier County. She was one of few female country music stars at the time, all produced and controlled by men in suits. It was such a man's world that she learned golf to keep in their loop.

According to her book, once she shot a birdie on a par three hole and was so proud she wanted to have the Titleist ball mounted. Wagoner said he would do it and then gave her a plaque without the special golf ball—it was an Arnold Palmer ball, instead. Parton described the incident as one of his many passive-aggressive digs.

Parton hadn't gotten tied down by some careless boy and a teenage pregnancy back in the woods. Instead, she wound up professionally and contractually bound to a man who fancied himself her husband, her father, her owner. That man happened to be her male counterpart in some ways—a talented, tenacious country kid with a guitar who worked hard and hit it big. What she'd stepped into was the wealthier, show business parallel of a life she'd meant to escape. Her songs from that period don't reflect the triumph of an individualistic woman who "got out" but rather the sorrows of women who weren't so lucky—a powerful statement of solidarity with her poor sisters back home but maybe, too, a coded revelation about her time with Porter Wagoner.

As Parton toured the country singing those songs, her bus might have passed women's protests, marches, sit-ins. Parton knew little of that world—direct political activism, an understanding of one's own agency in democracy, statistics and testimonies leveraged to change public policy. She did know what my grandma Betty knew: female life as a personal, intimate experience in which, at some point, an inner vibration you've been putting off will shake you so hard you'll fall to pieces if you don't leave.

That knowledge is something society will try to squash, because women who don't stay put cannot be controlled. All the institutions benefit if they stay: The heterosexual marriage, for which they carry laundry baskets and the emotional labor. The underpaying jobs, where they do their assigned tasks and are expected to organize the birthday cupcakes in the meeting room, too. The parenting, in which they still change most of the diapers regardless of who "brings home the bacon"—and they still fry most of the bacon, too.

"Stay," her small town probably told Parton when she left Tennessee in 1964, if only by pressuring her to become a wife and mother and laughing at her big ideas about becoming a star. "Stay," Porter Wagoner told her a decade later, in plain legal terms. In many ways that remains the message for women everywhere. But today we can revel in songs about leaving—songs telling stories that feel possible because of the exits women before us made.

A woman's departure is a declaration. Many of them—especially by the poor woman, the Black woman, the brown woman, the gay woman, the transgender woman—have gone unsung while more privileged people hold forth about equality at microphones next to capital buildings.

Dolly Parton had a different kind of microphone, and a woman her age named Betty was listening. I found Grandma Betty's old records when I was a kid, marked in pen with last names I didn't know she'd ever had. I was a child with ideas about leaving, and no one in my family or rural communities ever laughed when I said as much or tried to tell me that I couldn't. No one talked about "feminism" where I lived. But poor girls before me had already worn a groove in the highway.

AN OPEN DOOR

Parton's years with Wagoner bring to mind the first line from a famous 1978 poem by Adrienne Rich: "A wild patience has taken me this far." In that poem, by one of the country's eminent public intellectuals and second-wave feminists, the middle-aged speaker realizes her deepest strength is that she contains seemingly opposing attributes at once: anger and tenderness, a sad past and hope for the future, both pride and pain from having done a lifetime worth of work alone.

How can patience be wild? It is a question not unlike, "Why did you put up with it?" The latter insinuates that a strong woman wouldn't. But the fact is that, at least temporarily, almost every woman must.

Parton had gained economic stability from her business partnership with Wagoner. She was scandalously underpaid, of course. Like many working women today, though, on some level she was grateful and shocked to be paid at all.

"The jingles were sung, the smiles were faked, and the checks were cashed," Parton said in her autobiography. "Try to imagine what sixty thousand dollars represented to a young woman who had grown up in poverty in the Smoky Mountains. It was probably more than my daddy had earned in his lifetime."

Parton's first Christmas after she got the job on Wagoner's show, she re-did her parents' house with new furniture, drapes, carpet. Her younger siblings were still at home, and she made sure the girls had lots of the pink and frilly things Parton had longed for as a child. This concept of "girl stuff" might offend feminist thinking. The rub for Parton wasn't that such things were forced on her, though, but that she couldn't have them. In a place where women labored right alongside men, with no money for makeup or dresses even if they wanted them, pink ruffles weren't just a gender trap but an economic privilege.

(For the record, the first big purchase she says she made for herself, once she was thoroughly wealthy, wasn't girly stuff. It was a car—not a husband-approved Chevy but a Cadillac to her own liking.)

Grandma Betty never got rich or even became what many people would consider "comfortable," but her job in the

Kansas criminal justice system eventually provided enough that she could cover the bills while a small pension grew. When I was a kid, she had an emerald ring she always wore, and one day I asked her who had given it to her.

"I've had it since I started working in the courts," she told me. "I always wanted an emerald ring, so I bought the damn thing myself." She didn't need to explain to me the significance—that every other ring she'd put on a finger came from a man.

Through her gig on Wagoner's show, Parton got more than financial security. She racked up awards that had both their names on them; in 1968, they won the Country Music Association's honor for vocal group of the year. And Wagoner could be a real advocate for her when he wanted to be. Though their connection became strained, it had its good moments.

In 1970, Wagoner orchestrated "Dolly Parton Day" back in her hometown, bringing top Nashville musicians to Sevierville for the event. The performance was recorded for the essential live album *A Real Live Dolly*. Wagoner profited from that seemingly selfless tribute to Parton and her roots, of course, but by her account he had a genuine affection and respect for her, too. It was mutual.

"He was a Missouri boy with a dream," she wrote in her autobiography. Their life trajectories were so rare that they understood each other as few others were capable of understanding either one of them.

Wagoner could be a good teacher, too. By the time they became partners, she'd been working professionally for almost twenty years, since childhood. For entertaining a national audience, though, she still had a lot to learn.

"I could sing when I met Porter," Parton wrote. "After knowing him, I knew how to perform."

He taught her how to handle a ruckus in the audience; you can still see his mark on a Parton show today when someone interrupts a quiet moment with a shout and she throws back a line.

Parton might have acquired her taste for rhinestones and over-the-top hair from Wagoner, too; she has long been known to rock a Nudie suit.

Perhaps the most important impression Wagoner made on her, though, had to do with fans.

"Every night after performing on the road, no matter how small the town or seemingly insignificant the venue, Porter would stay and sign autographs until the last fan who wanted one had been satisfied," Parton recalled in her book.

As it happens, it was during one of those dedicated autograph sessions that she would have an encounter that paved the way for her to leave Wagoner. A little girl, nine or ten years old, held out a piece of paper to be signed. Parton admired her long, auburn hair.

"You sure are pretty," Parton would recall saying. "What's your name?"

"Jolene," the girl said.

Parton had never heard that name before. She remembered it a year later when, according to her, she sat down to write a song inspired by a flirtatious connection between her husband and an auburn-haired woman who worked at their bank. She needed a name for the character of the woman who represented a threat. The name she picked, plucked from that young fan she met while on the road with Wagoner, turned out to have such a ring to it that countless musicians across genres would cover the song for decades.

The 1973 single "Jolene" went to number one on the country charts, was a crossover pop success, and was nominated for a Grammy. It wasn't her first solo triumph, but something about the moment felt different.

Parton was emboldened. She had been patient over her years with Wagoner but never lost her own wild spirit. Despite the big smiles on camera and onstage, the pair had gone round and round behind the scenes.

"That was not unique to Porter," Parton wrote. "I had seldom agreed with parents, teachers, anybody who tried to exercise control over me, my talents, and my beliefs."

Ultimately, they had different visions: He wanted to keep her, and she wasn't for being kept.

"I guess the real problems that arose between Porter and me were all about dueling dreams," Parton wrote. "Porter dreamed of me staying with his show forever, and I dreamed of having my own show."

By then, she had been with the show for seven years—two years past her five-year contractual obligation—apparently from a sense of obligation to a man who claimed she owed him her career. Parton is not one to complain about or elaborate on her relationship with Wagoner as anything more than a blessing that often felt like a pain in the ass. But her jokes about those years, like the songs she wrote then, have a darkness to them.

"Looking back, it seems appropriate," she wrote of the time she stayed with Wagoner. "After all, the indentured servants who came to the New World had to work seven years for their freedom."

So in her late twenties, a decade after she left rural East Tennessee, she once again found the gumption to leave something that no longer served her purposes. They were on the road, touring as the longtime duet, Parton recalled in her book. There was a taxi in front of the hotel with the door opened for her.

"My knees nearly buckled, my heart nearly stopped, but I walked on," she wrote.

"When that car door closed, I knew it was the end of an era. One Dolly Parton had walked so painfully to the car and climbed inside; another stronger one had closed the door."

One of her concerns was that RCA wouldn't want her anymore. Wagoner, working cleverly as a go-between, had insinuated the label wasn't interested in her without him. She asked for a conference in New York and met with executives Ken Glancy and Mel Ilberman.

"I know I'm not the same without Porter," she recalled telling them, "but I'll be something really special by myself." According to Parton, they were shocked.

"We're somewhat interested in maintaining a relationship with Porter Wagoner, but we think you are the real star," they said.

It's hard to imagine a woman who would build a business empire feeling so unsure. It is no surprise, though, that she wouldn't know the world valued her as much as she valued herself. However strong you are, years of feedback from an emotional manipulator like Wagoner will do a number on your mind.

To mark her departure from the show, Parton wrote the tearjerker goodbye song "I Will Always Love You" and told Wagoner it was for him.

A song that powerful doesn't get written without truth behind every word. But consider what a goodbye in that form represented. No dummy, Parton had long ago established a song publishing company and retained the rights whenever someone recorded her work. Her bittersweet goodbye, thus, was something she owned and that Wagoner had no claim on. Every penny it earned fell into her account, not his.

Her first summer away from Wagoner, Parton hit the road to open for country singer Mac Davis. I imagine her rolling down the highway with her new band, Gypsy Fever, in a bus with butterflies and "Dolly" painted on the side. Riding along might have been Don Warden, the legendary steel guitarist who was from Wagoner's hometown and had been part of his show and original trio. He and Parton had become close; when she left Wagoner, so did he, to work as her manager for almost half a century.

Parton must have felt a new lightness as the bus zoomed past a field she wasn't working in, a diner where she would never have to wait tables. She was twenty-eight and free for the first time in her life, no place or man or contract pinning her wings. I imagine "I Will Always Love You" coming on the bus radio, the Gypsy Fever musicians cheering when the DJ announces it has hit number one on the charts. I imagine the 1972 Carly Simon hit "You're So Vain" playing next and Parton singing along, laughing her ass off at one particular line in the chorus: "I'll bet you think this song is about you, don't you?"

When Elvis Presley asked to record "I Will Always Love You," Parton was ecstatic, she recalled in a 2006 interview with CMT. She was a star by then, but Presley was already an icon. Then, at the last minute before the recording session, Presley's manager, "Colonel" Tom Parker, tried to pull a business maneuver on her.

"He said, 'Now you know we have a rule that Elvis don't record anything that we don't take half the publishing,'" Parton told CMT. "And I was really quiet. I said, 'Well, now it's already been a hit. I wrote it and I've already published it. And this is the stuff I'm leaving for my family when I'm dead and gone.'"

Parker told her it was deal or no deal.

"I guess they thought since they already had it prepared and already had it ready, that I would do it," Parton mused. "I said, 'I'm really sorry,' and I cried all night. . . . Other people were saying, 'You're nuts. It's Elvis Presley. I mean, hell, I'd give him all of it.'"

But Parton went with her gut. It would prove one of the most lucrative decisions of her life.

"I Will Always Love You" went to number one again when Parton re-recorded it in 1982, making it the only country song in history to top the charts in two separate decades. The song did it a third time, in 1992, when Whitney Houston made it a pop blockbuster on *The Bodyguard* soundtrack.

Thus, Parton's parting gift to the man who would have held her down ended up one of the most successful songs in music history. She is still cashing the checks.

"When Whitney's [version] came out, I made enough money to buy Graceland," Parton told CMT with a laugh.

The confidence to heed her inner voice and, in doing so, piss off a powerful man is what allowed Parton to leave Wagoner, say no to Elvis, and become not just a successful artist but also a business juggernaut.

"You need to really believe in what you've got to offer, what your talent is—and if you believe, that gives you strength," Parton told *Billboard* magazine in 2014. "In my early days, I would go in, and I was always over-made, with my boobs sticking out, my clothes too tight, and so I really looked like easy prey to a lot of guys—just looked easy, period. But I would go in, and if they were not paying close attention to what I was saying, I always said, 'I look like a woman, but I think like a man and you better pay attention or I'll have your money and I'll be gone.'"

Gone she was, and Wagoner responded with a bitter lawsuit. He claimed that, having played such a big role in her development, he was owed a cut of every profit she'd make for the rest of her life as an entertainer. That might seem like a losing claim today, but Parton had fair reason for concern as a woman facing the prospect of a courtroom with a male judge.

Rather than fight Wagoner in court, Parton offered to settle for a reported $1 million. Wagoner took the deal.

According to Parton's book, she didn't yet have that amount lying around and paid it off painstakingly over time. Meanwhile, Wagoner was slandering her any chance he could get.

"Dolly Parton is the kind of person that I would never trust with anything of mine," Wagoner told a TV interviewer in 1978. "I mean her family, her own blood, she would turn her back on to help herself. I'm not that kind of person." In spite of this, according to multiple sources, she sometimes bailed him out of tax trouble.

Parton and Wagoner would reconcile and reunite many times over the decades, even poking fun at their history together. At a 1995 roast of Wagoner, Parton told the crowd, "I knew he had balls when he sued me for a million dollars when he was only paying me thirty dollars a week."

Parton would continue to reflect on Wagoner with a mix of straight talk and gracious thanks over the years.

"I will always be grateful to Porter, because I learned a lot," she told *Rolling Stone* in 2003. "But he got as much out of me as I got out of him, let's put it that way. Porter was very much like my dad and my brothers and the men I grew up with. They were just manly men, and a woman's place was where you told her to be. And so I would always stand up to him. . . . And we fought like hell, and he showed his ass about it, rather than just letting life flow. He had to sue me. And, of course, that broke both our hearts. And, you know, looking back on it now, he hates that he did that and has said so."

Parton and Wagoner might have buried the hatchet, but even his 2007 obituary in the *New York Times* revealed Wagoner's selfish nature:

"For all Mr. Wagoner's accomplishments, he could not escape a certain question. 'Did you sing with Dolly?' too many people asked.

" 'No,' he would say with a smile. 'She sang with me.' "

PUNCHING OUT

As Parton was leaving Wagoner, feminist activism was changing the world. The Supreme Court ruled on *Roe v. Wade*, which might have saved so many of the young, pregnant, abandoned protagonists of Parton's early songs, in 1973. The next year, mandatory unpaid maternity leave became illegal, and the Women's Educational Equity Act funded development of less sexist teaching materials.

While many of those gains have been lasting, the United States did not emerge into some bright, easy moment for women. Reproductive rights, in particular, have been the target of death-by-a-thousand-cuts political strategies for decades.

Similarly, though freed from her chains to Wagoner, Parton did not find herself in a pat, happy ending. A woman can leave the poor countryside and a domineering male boss, but she can't leave a culture of sexism and misogyny. Mindfully reject it every single day with some success? Perhaps. Exist outside it? No.

To say nothing of battles she surely fought behind closed doors, Parton's songwriting would continue to outrage powerful men well past the moment at which equality had supposedly been reached. Her 1991 song "Eagle When She Flies," a ballad she wrote to pay homage to the simultaneous vulnerability and deep power of women, had trouble getting on the airwaves just like "Down from Dover" and "The Bargain Store" had a quarter century prior.

"Lots of DJs wouldn't play [it] because they thought it was such a women's lib song," Parton recalled in the 2003 *Rolling Stone* interview.

That Parton herself didn't affix the label "women's lib" to her own work tells you where she came from. But the fact that men decided her song shouldn't be heard tells you exactly what it was.

Parton's response to male DJs chucking "Eagle When She Flies": She performed it at the Country Music Association

Awards with president George H. W. Bush and First Lady Barbara Bush in the front row. She took the opportunity to introduce her song using no less than the ultimate symbol of patriarchy—the rich, white, male leader of the world—as a contrast with what she hoped to exalt.

"Everybody was talkin' about how proud we are to have the president here. And we are. Very honored. But I wanted to do a song tonight, and I want to dedicate this to Barbara Bush," Parton said, her platinum wig almost as high as some of her old beehives and her neckline much lower than what Porter Wagoner would have approved. "We know there are some wonderful men in this world, but there are equally as many great women. She and people like her and women from all walks of life. . . . So this is for all the women here tonight and everywhere."

The stage lit up to reveal a large, mostly white choir in cheesy outfits representing professional trades women were newly entering—the businesswoman in shoulder pads, the delivery driver in a brown jumpsuit holding a box, the soldier in fatigues, the astronaut, policewoman, surgeon, construction worker, even a movie director. The jobs that previously had been occupied by women were there, too—the teacher, the nurse, the rancher, the diner waitress with her tray. But the president of the United States of America, a man who had everything handed to him while Parton earned hers, had to consider the visuals. Captive before cameras in the front row, he watched as the daughter of an illiterate farmer told him his wife was his equal. It was an exquisite demonstration that, for all its goofy imagery, still feels radical when you watch it today.

That was almost thirty years after Parton left Sevierville, Tennessee, as a teenager with a guitar. By the time of that CMA Awards performance, sexual discrimination in the workplace was against the law, and more women were recording country music. In many ways, women have made even more progress since then. But some of us get so lost in the policy-centered discussion of feminism that we fail to look ruthlessly at the way we live our lives. What sort of country songs might be written about us? Would they be about the woman who is stuck or the one breaking free?

You might know a well-off woman with a college degree and a friendly, philandering husband who pays the bills but treats her like a trophy or a maid whether she has her own job or not. She might be comfortable enough in her life to remain. She might even wear a T-shirt that reads "feminist" while she picks up her husband's dry cleaning. She might know terms that a poor woman can't define, and she might type an outraged post on Facebook about our misogynist president.

Meanwhile, a woman in poverty is walking out some door with nothing to her name, to start over yet again, in the hopes that she and her children will find some goddamn respect. The woman who speaks about feminism is not always the one truly insisting on equality behind closed doors.

Whether penniless Dolly Parton refusing to stay in a holler or affluent Dolly Parton looking at the door of Porter Wagoner's studio, leaving was a revolutionary act. It is a power that has, over the years, brought textile mills, coal companies, and rich corporations to their knees when gender and poverty intersect and working women have had enough.

I recall the thrill I felt as a child watching an episode of *Roseanne* in which the title character stands up to a sexist, verbally abusive boss who goes back on his word and reinstates brutal production quotas for female employees at a plastics plant in small-town Illinois.

"You'll stay . . . and so will your loser friends," the boss tells her. After some hot words, Roseanne storms off to the factory floor.

"Hey, I'm not done with you!" he yells and follows her to where the other women are moving plastic pieces. "Roseanne, I thought I told you not to walk away from me."

"I'm walking away from you forever," she says, her voice soft like she is scared. "I'm walking away from this stinking factory. I'm walking away from this lousy job." Roseanne punches her timecard.

"Well, that was a wonderful performance, Roseanne," he says. "If any of you are considering joining her, may I point out there are two doors to this room. One that pays, and one that doesn't."

One by one, her friends of different races and ages stand up and punch their cards.

When Parton punched her card and walked out of the Porter Wagoner music factory, she was helping make a path for female artists in an industry where they still rarely head-lined a show.

"There was Patsy Cline and Loretta and Tammy and me," Parton told *Rolling Stone*. "There were just very few of us, and they were all under the direction of men."

You might have seen that list of names before in big letters on a trendy T-shirt sometimes worn by young women: "Dolly & Loretta & Patsy & Tammy," the shirt reads.

When you see it, if you're able, consider it a reminder to give a big tip to the next woman who serves you at a diner like the ones on the Great Plains where my grandma waited tables, or to the cleaning lady carrying a bucket on and off Grey-hound buses like Cline used to do down South. Feminism owes her a debt, and there's a good chance she's saving up to get somewhere. Her life isn't the kind you want to lean into.

PART THREE

DOLLY PARTON BECOMES THE BOSS

PART THREE

DOLLY PARTON BECOMES THE BOSS

— FALL 2017 —

In the 1980 movie *9 to 5*, three fed-up women take on the male boss who berates, gropes, and demeans them. A parable imparting lessons for men and women alike, the movie was for many viewers the first articulation and condemnation of flagrantly, dangerously sexist office culture that had long been accepted as "the way things are" or "boys being boys."

For Dolly Parton, playing the boss's objectified secretary wasn't a stretch. Just a few years prior, she had quit *The Porter Wagoner Show*, where she had spent years on the payroll of one of Nashville's most infamous male egos.

"I know all about bosses from Porter Wagoner," Parton told *Entertainment Weekly* in 2009, after writing the score for *9 to 5*'s Broadway adaptation. "He was a male chauvinist pig too."

Perhaps that is why, of the three powerhouse female leads— Parton, Jane Fonda, and Lily Tomlin—the least accomplished actress gives, for my money, the most convincing portrayal.

Fonda and Tomlin knew sexism, of course. And Tomlin,

the daughter of a factory worker who—as Parton's father briefly did—left the South for steady work in Detroit, surely knew firsthand the intersections of gender and economic strife. But something sparkles about Parton on-screen, in particular, and it's not just her frosted eye shadow.

It's that she was entering the apex of her career—a period in which she would become not only a movie star but a business magnate and global icon. She would do it all sporting a huge platinum-blond wig, skin-tight clothes, and ample cleavage.

She was, perhaps, a third-wave feminist born a generation early, simultaneously defying gender norms and reveling in gender performance before that was a political act. Country girls like me were watching.

I recently attended a screening of *9 to 5* in an Austin, Texas, theater full of women shouting at the screen. People think of the film as a comedy, and that's how I had remembered it from TV airings when I was a kid. But rewatching it as a woman, I felt a wave of trauma-triggered nausea overcome me when Parton's character is physically grabbed by her boss. Women in the audience cheered when the lead characters fantasize about murder and laugh when they stuff what they think is their boss's dead body into the trunk of a car. I realized it is one of the darkest movies ever made about the female experience.

It is also, still, painfully relevant. Thirty-six years after the film's release, the US president embodies the disgusting male boss. Starring in a reality show in which he got off on delivering the words "you're fired," Donald Trump infamously told a female contestant she would look good on her knees. Contestants in the beauty pageants he owned have reported that he had a habit of walking in while they were changing clothes. In these times, *9 to 5* feels so political that one wonders whether it would be greenlighted by a major studio today.

Born the same year *9 to 5* was released, I am now about the age that Parton was when she starred in the film. I also happen to be what, during my 1980s childhood and 1990s adolescence, people still called "a professional woman"— financially independent since age eighteen by the sweat of my own brow, happily divorced and childless, more driven by career goals than domestic ones.

I have come to think of myself and similar women of my generation as *9 to 5*'s cultural offspring. We were formed in a confusing soup of new social freedoms and old expectations. Society was embracing a new vision of the modern woman: She left in the morning to work as a doctor, an engineer, a police officer. But did she also like to bake? Of course, it's possible to love to cook, wear high heels, and do all manner of stereotypically "feminine" things and be no less a feminist for it. Mainstream culture seems to be clear on that today. But the defining friction for women in the late twentieth century was being encouraged to become whatever they wanted, even as they were criticized no matter how they went about it. If they charged into the male-dominated halls of business or government, their feminism made them shrill Amazons in the eyes of threatened men; if they wore low-cut shirts and tight pants while making empowered decisions, their feminism was missed altogether in the eyes of threatened women.

The idea of gender equality both at home and at work was so new then that a woman's entire life could be experienced as an intentional corrective for centuries of unfair treatment. A little more than a decade after *9 to 5*'s release, in 1992, the first lady of Arkansas—a Yale Law School–educated attorney named Hillary Clinton—caught hell for telling reporters covering her husband's presidential campaign why she worked on public policy rather than draperies as the wife of a governor.

"I suppose I could have stayed home and baked cookies and had teas," Clinton said. "But what I decided to do was to fulfill my profession, which I entered before my husband was in public life." That quote, and widespread pearl-clutching in response to it, would continue to haunt her twenty-four years later when she ran for president herself.

Clinton spoke snidely about baking cookies not because she hates to bake but because for centuries society has handed women aprons while begrudging them social and political power. Parton fashioned herself as a "floozy" not because she sought men's approval but because sexualizing herself took control from men who otherwise would have done it for her.

In the herky-jerky social gains that unfolded at the end of the last century, women had no choice but for their actions to be reactions. It is a conundrum inherent to any sort of disadvantage, if one means to fight it. In *9 to 5*, the female leads aren't homicidal criminals by nature. They don't *want* to kill their boss. But they find that perhaps they must.

According to original screenwriter Patricia Resnick, her first version of the script was even more macabre. In a 2015 interview with *Rolling Stone* marking the movie's thirty-fifth anniversary, Resnick said she had wanted to make "a very dark comedy in which the secretaries actually tried to kill the boss." Those plot points were rewritten as fantasy sequences in the interest of the three protagonists' likability.

As for general casting, that the lead actresses would all be white probably wasn't even questioned. A woman of color rarely headlines a film to this day, much less as a character pointing a gun at a white male boss.

Something else that hasn't changed is the relevance of the gender points the movie made. Resnick recalled conversations with skeptical media when the movie was turned into a Broadway production in 2009.

"It was really frustrating," she said, "because a lot of the interviews that I did with male journalists, the first thing they said was 'Well, none of those issues are a problem in contemporary life, so how are women of today going to be able to relate to it?' I thought, yeah, you can't sexually harass someone as obviously. We don't call people 'secretaries.' Other than that, what has changed?"

As a woman who has held many jobs in the workforce over the course of more than twenty years and never—not once—worked somewhere without some sort of harassment or other poor treatment for my gender, I must say that I agree. The relentless emotional drain of being dismissed, underpaid, ogled, and perceived as a threat is no small part of why I now sacrifice the many benefits and securities of organizational structure in order to work as a freelance writer.

What's different for me and my generation than it was for our mothers and grandmothers, as Resnick describes, is that many of the men who have antagonized us in workplaces did so in ways much quieter than *9 to 5*'s bombastic chauvinism—often while purporting to be "feminists." That can be an even more dangerous professional climate for women; insidious misogyny or sexism can cut you before you see it and is the hardest to prove.

Feminism and all movements for social progress inevitably contain a gap between what's on paper and what's really going on: between the feminism proclaimed and the feminism enacted, the women's rights legislated and the women's rights enforced, the progress in policy and the progress in culture. Women of Generation X, of which I represent the youngest contingent, had more freedom than their mothers in meaningful ways. We were the first full beneficiaries of Title IX protections guaranteeing access to education and outlawing sexual discrimination in the workplace. We were entering our first romantic partnerships as the Violence Against Women Act became law. But the cultural cues we received growing up were full of gaps and dissonance.

I was recently stunned by an old episode of *Moonlighting*, a favorite childhood show that in my memory was a feminist triumph for featuring Cybill Shepherd as a whip-smart (and damn funny) detective. Bruce Willis's character, the smirking work partner with whom she has just ended an on-again/off-again romance, appears in her house against her will. He refuses to leave when she tells him to, slaps her in the face for arguing with him—and then is welcomed into her arms for his relentlessness.

My twentieth-century child eyes had seen a strong woman

putting up a fight and then being turned on by a man persistent enough to win. But my twenty-first-century adult eyes saw a dangerously entitled man stalking a woman and not respecting or even believing her when she said "no."

That was the confusion *9 to 5* articulated at the start of the 1980s: a woman's new role in the economy at cross purposes, in men's eyes, with her old role in bed. Female Baby Boomers faced it, and their Generation X daughters watched them come home ragged in high heels and with little time to complain.

Those same woes affect women today and will do so for generations to come. But *9 to 5* represents a specific moment of tension in feminism's evolution: The Equal Rights Amendment hadn't yet been squashed, middle-class women were power-walking to work (as poor women had been doing all along), and popular culture revealed a deep collective crisis about gender.

That decade of transition—from the Carter era to the Reagan, from polyester bell bottoms to stone-washed denim, from women's-lib signs to the incorrect presumption that liberation had occurred—marked an epic shift in Parton's career, too. Having established herself as a solo country-music star as a young woman in the 1970s, *9 to 5* turned her into a mainstream Hollywood superstar and accelerated her toward becoming an icon.

Parton never leveraged her celebrity at feminist marches or in overt political action. But she did choose as her first script, among what must have been numerous options, a movie conceived by one of the most vilified feminists of the time—Jane Fonda, then still a divisive figure with her anti-war "Hanoi Jane" controversy fresh in national memory. And Parton accepted as her first role a character who lassoes her abusive boss and shoves a pistol in his face.

Surely it's no accident that Parton was eager to play Doralee, the pretty secretary both sexually harassed by her repugnant male boss and ostracized by her female co-workers, who spread the false rumor that she was sleeping with him.

Doralee's particular affliction among the other mistreated female workers was being deemed a "slut" because of her sexy appearance and other men's false claims that they were banging her. Parton herself got used to that in high school.

"I wore a lot of makeup. I wore real tight clothes, and I wore my hair a mile high. I looked like the real trash that a lot of the girls were," Parton told David Letterman on the *Late Show* in 1987. "A lot of those people thought I was a bad influence on their daughters 'cause I told jokes and I wore a lot of makeup. Actually I was pretty good. I just had a real outgoing personality. Some of the girls I was hanging around with were really doing it, and I was gettin' all the credit for it."

FEMINIST SWEET SPOT

In spite of the era's mixed messages, I feel fortunate to have come of age during the feminist sweet spot after the organized marches and policy triumphs of the 1970s but before the full-throated conservative backlash of the new millennium. After *Roe v. Wade* but before right-wing zealots created a successful policy strategy for chipping away at reproductive rights. After women entered traditionally male occupations en masse but before internet trolls harnessed technology to stalk, harass, and shame them. After female journalists began hosting national network shows but before Fox News put their legs in the shot.

Women my age—children and adolescents in the eighties, teenagers and young women in the nineties—may remember that time more through its records, cassette tapes, and television-channel dials than for its adult politics. But what we found through those albums and TV series often had a decidedly political undercurrent.

Our most formative years came before the hot-pink, baby-talk girl power of the Spice Girls and Britney Spears and the overt, unapologetic embrace of the term "feminism" by Beyoncé and the Dixie Chicks. We had instead a slew of tough bitches in pantsuits, running intellectual circles around the men they worked with: Murphy Brown, Dana Scully. In big, angular hairdos, delivering the nightly news: Connie Chung, Diane Sawyer. In shoulder pads on their way out the door as elegant but take-no-crap working moms: Clair Huxtable, Angela Bower. In leather jackets, singing pop songs in which they embodied a streetwise sexual power: Whitney Houston, Selena. In baggy pants and sneakers, rapping demands for respect: Queen Latifah, Salt-N-Pepa. And in combat boots telling the world to absolutely fuck off: Shirley Manson, Sinéad O'Connor.

As for pop-country music, a genre increasingly associated with conservatism, that period featured women in rhinestones and fringed leather singing triumphantly about hard-won independence.

On the Judds's chart-topping 1984 debut album, *Why Not Me*, perhaps my mother's most frequently spun vinyl record when I was a little kid, "Girls' Night Out" expresses relief at the end of a long work week. "I've been cooped up all week long / I've been workin' my fingers to the bone," the Judds sing over saloon piano and steel guitar. They're heading out to dance and party and close down the country bar.

That's it. That's the whole song—fun for their own sake, no mention of finding a man.

In another catchy song my mom played over and over in the tape deck of her car, 1987's "Younger Men," K. T. Oslin declares that she has started entertaining younger lovers. She recalls laughing, as a young woman, at a statistic about men reaching their sexual peak at age nineteen and women at forty. Oslin sings, "Now I'm staring forty right in the face / And the only trouble with being a woman my age is the men my age."

My mom was only in her mid-twenties when that album, *80's Ladies,* came out. I was all of seven. But as Mom cruised down the road with a Marlboro Light between her fingers and I bobbed my head in the passenger seat, we both relished talking along with the song's spoken aside. Oslin herself is behind the wheel, flipping the usual gender roles of catcaller in the vehicle and catcallee on the sidewalk: "Blue shorts, no shirt / WOOOO you're lookin' good, darlin'! / That's right—stay in shape."

Once we were singing along with that song when, my hand to God, we drove past a man jogging in blue shorts, and we both cracked up—a blissful surge of empowerment coursing through us from Oslin's songwriting pen to a busted road in Kansas. I'm not sure how either of us resonated with the particular power reversal in a middle-aged woman singing those words, but a twenty-something mom and her precocious daughter somehow already understood.

Parton was middle-aged by then, too, and had been ahead of the times in writing songs about sexual power. As the 1970s wound down, she began shifting her lyrics away from the broken, wronged women her earlier career documented to up-tempo songs like the pop-country hit "Two Doors Down" from the disco-inflected 1978 album *Here You Come Again.*

In the song, the woman singing is crying over something—presumably a breakup—but decides to stop moping around. She hears a rager going on down the hallway and moseys in that direction. By the next verse, she's asking a new guy to come back to her place. Parton sings, "Here we are feeling everything but sorry / We're having our own party two doors down."

Parton, who made a home in Los Angeles in 1976, surely was influenced by the sexual liberation messages of that period's counterculture movement. But she has described feeling that same freedom and power as a teenager in rural Tennessee—self-possession before society approved.

Having married soon after arriving in Nashville at age eighteen in 1964, the extent to which Parton's sexual experience was or wasn't contained by monogamous marriage is for her to know. ("I said I was married," she told the *New York Times* in 2016. "I didn't say I was dead.") But the garish 1980s saw her exaggerating and emphasizing her appearance in new ways that suggest a woman truly coming into her own, sexually. Down went her neckline, up went her heels.

After portraying misunderstood Doralee in *9 to 5*, in 1982 Parton starred alongside Burt Reynolds as the archetypal heart-of-gold sex worker in *The Best Little Whorehouse in Texas.* It's worth noting that in the brothel she's no longer a worker bee but rather the queen. The metaphor of the downtrodden working girl, though, is one that would always inflect her worldview.

"When I think somebody's acting more like a pimp than a manager, and I'm more of a prostitute than an artist, I always tell them where to put it," Parton told *Maclean's* in 2014. "People will use you as long as you let them."

The feminism in Parton's music and persona might have been lost on cultural critics of the day, but behind the scenes it was hard to miss. While in Austin the year *Best Little Whorehouse* was released, Parton asked to meet firebrand Texas liberal Ann Richards, who was making her first run for state treasurer.

When they met at the storied Driskill Hotel in downtown Austin, photographer Scott Newman was shooting a campaign event for Richards. He snapped a photograph of the women standing together: Richards, a progressive known for flagrant feminism and terrific one-liners, and Parton, a new movie star known for her version of the same thing.

In the black-and-white photo, the two women are in profile, overwhelmed with joyful laughter and near mirror images but for difference in age and body shape: blond, tight curls atop both their heads and ruffles on both their tops.

"What a scene to witness!" Newman wrote in the notes for

a recent exhibition of his photography. "These two women, two of my all-time favorite human beings, took such delight in each other."

Parton and Richards would become great friends and were both on their way up: Parton to becoming a pop culture icon and Richards to becoming, as of this writing, the last woman and the last Democrat to govern the state of Texas. Two different paths, but two women with much in common.

The Lone Star State, as well as country music and indeed the entire country, has changed a lot in the more than three decades since that picture was taken. Texas and the rest of the country has swung right; one doubts Ann Richards would win a Texas race today. Meanwhile, Nashville has shunned female political renegades like the Dixie Chicks while embracing a slew of male stars, from "bro country" Luke Bryan to old-school, bearded outlaw Chris Stapleton. Country radio stopped playing Parton's new music decades ago. It's hard to imagine the Southern gothic defenses of poor women she penned in her twenties making it on the air today.

But there in that 1982 photograph, in a Southern state capital, is the brief but powerful juncture in American history that girls like me—then a toddler living in a metal trailer on the Kansas prairie—somehow absorbed. A female politician and a female country-superstar-gone-Hollywood, exchanging looks of mutual respect, throwing back their heads and laughing in the public space of power that reactionary twenty-first-century misogyny had not yet spread its male legs to reclaim.

BODY POLITICS

Reactions to her physical shape meant that Parton didn't have much choice in carrying a hyper-awareness of her form and its relationship to the world. Every woman suffers under the male gaze, but Parton's experience reveals how invisible a woman's humanity might be rendered when that gaze is a laser beam the size of Earth.

When she went on *The Tonight Show* in 1977, Johnny Carson, whose persona was something of a gentleman, stammered and said, "I have certain guidelines on this show, but I would give about a year's pay to peek under [her top]."

She couldn't even escape being made a visual object, of sorts, by a blind man. In 1978, at the awards show where she became the second woman ever to be named the Country Music Association Entertainer of the Year (now one of seven, total), visually impaired singer Ronnie Milsap told the crowd, "I want to know why she wasn't in my braille *Playboy.*" (Parton had appeared on the cover of that month's issue of the magazine in a bunny outfit but had refused to pose nude.)

In her 1994 autobiography, *Dolly*, Parton describes the

pressures she faced during that time without pointing out the gendered component to all of them: male business associates with bad advice, her siblings' resentment for her fame and fortune in spite of her generosity as a family caretaker, Hollywood's sexist body-shaming.

The shoot for *Best Little Whorehouse* was particularly miserable, Parton wrote, citing the set's generally bad vibe. Her small but voluptuous shape was considered fat for the big screen. Parton's account of being embarrassed while shooting take after take of a scene in which Reynolds's character picks her up to carry her over a threshold is wince-inducing. In recalling the experience, she focuses on her own responsibility in the scene, admitting she felt like a failure for her weight.

Parton's impoverished childhood, during which deprivation and hunger helped form her psyche, complicated her relationship to the already troubled matter of a woman's appetite and body size.

"My daddy and mama, they just think I'm dyin' or somethin'," Parton told Chantal Westerman on a 1987 *Good Morning America* segment soon after she became noticeably thinner (much to the media's obsession). ". . . At home, my daddy always says, 'If you're gainin' weight, you're pickin' up. And if you're losin' weight, you're fallin' off.' So Daddy said, 'Boy, you're fallin' off. You're still fallin' off, aintcha?'"

Her father spent decades farming and working construction to ensure his eleven surviving children didn't starve to death. While Parton has pointed out that she's not underweight for a petite woman, and her "dramatic weight loss" in the eighties was, for her, a shift to feeling more healthy rather than less, a culture and family shaped by the Great Depression and even the European famines their ancestors fled will see shrinking size as potential cause for alarm.

Meanwhile, as Carson's and Milsap's quips document, what culture did to reconcile the confounding matter of Dolly Parton—a quick mind, a pretty face, a creative genius, and a huge rack all rolled into one—was to make her the punch line of a joke about big tits.

That joke became so pervasive in the American consciousness that I recall being a child on a playground in the 1980s watching little boys put balls under their shirts and say, "Look, I'm Dolly Parton." Or, "What's this?" they'd ask and turn their hands upside down with just the middle finger extended. (Answer: "Dolly Parton standing behind a tree.")

Parton reclaimed the joke; you'll often find her referencing her own bosom before anyone else has a chance to. She built a career on that sort of spirit. But it must have been a perilous emotional journey to gain command over the forces that sought to diminish her.

Not long after she "lost the weight" that decade, Parton had breast augmentation surgery, which she has discussed in general terms in her book and elsewhere. Photos from early in her career show that, while her breasts might now be termed "fake," they're about the same size they were when they were "real." People find the resulting figure—a tiny woman with breasts that don't seem to match her size—shocking. But it makes sense that a woman whose mere mention provoked boob jokes might reclaim not just the joke but the boob itself—as if to make clear, perhaps, that no punch line had caused her to feel shame.

Parton always smiled and laughed when asked about the hard juxtaposition of her childhood in poverty, her career as a musician and business owner, and her celebrity as a female sex symbol. But such forces take a toll, even on a woman who "made it" because of her natural grit.

It was a painful time for the women who blazed the trail Parton was on—a trail most blocked and treacherous for women of color, gay women, and others outside the cisgender, straight, white mold more palatable to American systems of power. For any woman on that path, the decade was a cluster of mixed messages: Work a "man's job" but for less pay than men. Wear shoulder pads to evoke a man's strength but also high heels to click delicately down the hallway. Be independent enough to drive to the office but answer to a male boss and cook your husband's dinner when you both get home from work.

That mess of expectations has changed little in the last thirty years, but in the 1980s it had a newness that left American culture spinning and drove even tough-as-nails Parton to collapse. Such a woman often pays a severe price, because in her world she is everyone else's support system. Who, then, looks after her?

In the early 1980s, when Parton was in her thirties, she experienced her darkest period: a physical and emotional breakdown during which she pondered suicide. Her personal crash happened to coincide with the anti-feminist backlash's first big victory—defeat of the Equal Rights Amendment in 1982.

Parton's book names her longtime agent and intimate Sandy Gallin, the late talent shepherd who also helmed Michael Jackson's career, as a source of nurturing guidance to help her through her severe depression. Ultimately, though, Parton had to do what so many women must in order to find a life that suits them rather than everyone around them: Burn it all down and rebuild.

Around that time, Parton fired some associates, including band members and an accounting firm that kept forgetting that she called the shots with her own money. She also had a partial hysterectomy, she has said without completely outlining the reasons. One welcome result she has noted was getting off the excessive-estrogen birth control pills then on the market. It was also a moment of finality about her choice not to have children.

After cleaning house in her business, her band, her cupboards, her bloodstream, and even her own womb, Parton rebounded from the emotional collapse. Her thoughts got more positive, her body came into balance, and her business began a crescendo that hasn't stopped since.

She didn't need to kill herself, she wrote in her book, because she'd experienced what some cultures call a shamanic death. "By the grace of God," she wrote, "I had [died] without experiencing it in the actual physical sense."

Parton had been actively, consciously evolving since adolescence—from a poor country girl to a Nashville hopeful, from Porter Wagoner's micromanaged co-star to crossover solo artist, from small-town singer to big-screen actress. Now she'd achieved the level of fame and fortune she'd hustled toward all her life, bottomed out emotionally, and found herself the same woman she'd always been—yet psychologically reborn. What would be the next goal? She had conquered a man's world the best a woman could and found it a place that would treat her like dirt even when she was on top. There was only one thing left to do: create her own damn world.

WELCOME TO DOLLYWOOD

"I never got to go to Disneyland as a child, but I was always fascinated with it," Parton told *Maverick* magazine in 2011, twenty-five years after opening an amusement park in her native Smoky Mountains. In the 1980s, as a homesick, newly minted movie star disgusted with the Hollywood she dreamed of as a child, Parton had returned to the Smokies to create a place called Dollywood.

Dollywood theme park wasn't just a selfish enterprise. It was her vision for energizing her home's ailing rural economy and putting its people—including her own family members—to work.

"I knew it would be a great place for all the hardworkin', good-hearted, honest people in this area that don't have jobs," she told *Maverick*. It would be a joyful place, she imagined, full of fun, music, rides, craftsmanship, and culture reflecting her native region.

"A lot of my businesspeople said: 'That's a big mistake, that is a great way to lose all your money,'" Parton told Reuters in 2016. "But I had a feeling in my stomach that it was the right thing to do, so I went ahead with it. Then I got rid of those lawyers and accountants who didn't believe in me and got new ones who did."

Parton was the boss now, and her business instincts were

right. She told Reuters that Dollywood, which celebrated its thirtieth anniversary in 2016, is the most lucrative investment she ever made. Three million people visit annually. Adding to Parton's satisfaction, and indeed to the park's success, is that multiple generations of her own kin continue to work and perform at the attraction, as she once envisioned.

Parton's goals for Dollywood's community impact came to fruition, too. Along with two related attractions, the Pigeon Forge, Tennessee, tourist magnet employs about thirty-five hundred people and creates nearly twenty thousand jobs in the area, according to a study by University of Tennessee researchers this year. Dollywood's annual economic impact on East Tennessee, according to the researchers, is $1.5 billion. (Yes, that's billion.) Had Parton listened to the people who doubted her business savvy, it's not only she who would have lost out on financial returns but an entire state.

Amid the launch of that venture, Parton managed to record one of the greatest collaborative albums of all time, 1987's *Trio*, with Emmylou Harris and Linda Ronstadt. *Trio*, which features incredible harmonies and defiantly country sound, won a Grammy and topped the *Billboard* country albums chart.

That same year, Parton hosted a new TV show for ABC. This time it was Parton pooh-poohing someone else's ideas, and for good reason: They sucked. Network television executives forced stupid, awkward skits onto the show, *Dolly*, which she had hoped would be a bigger-budget version of the show of the same name that she hosted in Nashville in the 1970s. That earlier show had focused on her natural gifts for music, storytelling, and organic conversation with guests. But ABC insisted, for instance, that each episode of her new show open with her taking a bubble bath on camera. She described the experience of working with a roomful of male writers and producers in her book *Dolly*:

"I was naïve enough to think that what I wanted would somehow matter to the people in network television . . ." she wrote. "Sometimes I would hear things brought up and I would wait for everybody to laugh at how ridiculous it was, but the laugh never came. The laugh was on me when the ridiculous idea actually got done."

On *Good Morning America* in 1987, when co-host Charlie Gibson interviewed her about her new show's struggling ratings, Parton defended herself and her hopes for the show.

"We're just kind of weedin' out what ain't workin' really well, which is mostly things I didn't think would work to start with," Parton told Gibson. "Everybody's just trying a little too hard, I think. . . . The people don't know what to make of it. 'Why are you taking a bubble bath on television?' I asked that myself. But anyway, you do what you gotta do."

Dignified newsman Gibson's non sequitur in response: "The hair may be false, but everything else is real, right?"

In the segment, Gibson never offered a chance for her to plug her work. So, after he cued her farewell, instead of saying goodbye, Parton listed her upcoming show's guests, including Patti LaBelle.

"Not to run through the whole cast or anything," Gibson condescended. "Thanks very—"

"Well, I might as well—that's what I'm on television for," Parton interrupted with an incredulous smile and raised eyebrows. "You didn't think I got up just to say hello to you, did ya?"

"Absolutely that's what I thought," Gibson shot back with a similarly tense smile, and Parton talked over him again.

"I got up to advertise," she said.

That same year, in a rare occurrence of a member of the press discussing Parton's wit rather than her body, *Washington Post* reporter Jacqueline Trescott incorporated another Parton exchange into a story about new-hire Gibson's flat presence next to *Good Morning America* co-host Joan Lunden.

"Some show business pros are quicker than he is," wrote Trescott. "When he asked entertainer Parton if she had tested the water slide at her theme park, Dollywood, she said, 'It's no kind of ride for a woman with a hairdo like mine.' Gibson gamely moved on to her successful diet and asked her waistline measurement. Parton replied, 'Between 18 and 23. People think I am big busted but it is because I squish it all in.' Then he asked her about her lucrative contract with ABC to produce a series of variety shows and she replied, 'It takes a lot of money to make a person look this cheap.'

"Swallowing his comebacks, as the control room collapsed in convulsions, Gibson signed off, 'Thanks ever so much.'"

Parton got the last laugh about her TV show, too. Thanks to a well-negotiated contract, ABC had to pay her millions to cancel the show when it tanked. She also walked away with a deepened wisdom about the business world, which—in a rare instance of overriding her natural diplomacy and going for the throat—she outlined in *Dolly: My Life and Other Unfinished Business*. Don't assume the men in suits know what they're doing, she warned, and don't concern yourself with their appraisal of your worth.

". . . Although the ratio may be better than in some other businesses, show business is still essentially a man's world," Parton wrote. "As a woman, that can be difficult to deal with. Especially if you are a five-foot-two blonde with a hick accent. In addition, the difficulty factor is multiplied by two for every cup size."

Parton's professional strategy in response to that difficulty was to play it to her own advantage.

"There are basically two kinds of men you have to deal with in business: the ones who want to screw you out of money, and the ones who want to screw you, period," she wrote. "I should point out that I am not interested in screwing anybody [professionally]. I never want anything more than what's fair. The problem is, I never want anything less either. In the old-boy school of business, if a woman walks away from the table with what's rightfully hers, the man feels screwed anyway. I have to admit that adds to the satisfaction of making a fair deal. 'How was it for you, old boy?' "

As the eighties waned, Parton was in full bloom as the woman we know today: a smart business shark with a hyper-sexualized physical presentation curated for her own power and delight. What man's head did she need to turn by that point? She was on the back side of forty and had long been the boss.

Her 1989 music video for "Why'd You Come in Here Lookin' Like That," from her classic album *White Limozeen,* is a cheesy but delightfully meta staging of auditions for the male lead in a music video. She didn't happen to write that number-one hit, which laments how fine a bad boy's ass looks in "painted-on jeans" and which she still performs with conviction at age seventy-one. But in the video, she's in charge, watching from a dark theater seat with the house lights down as men walk on stage, flex their muscles, and represent caricatures of various sorts of jerks. She laughs and loves them anyway. ("I think they're all real sweet," she tells the casting director when he asks for her thoughts.) Her reward for her Christian patience: A perfectly chiseled janitor in cowboy boots and a cut-off denim shirt accidentally walks into the spotlight with a push broom. Perhaps in answer to Charlie Gibson, Johnny Carson, Ronnie Milsap, and all the powerful, famous men who ignored her artistry in favor of discussing her body, Parton looks the janitor up and down as if to say, "You're hired."

MEDIA SCRUTINY

In 1983, when Parton visited the UK for a TV special called *Dolly in London*, a male reporter at a press conference asked her if it were true that she didn't consider herself a sex symbol. She explained that she dressed the way she did not as a gimmick but because she was "impressed with the people back home"—a reference to "trashy" women whose makeup and hair dye she once coveted in a rural community where few women had access to such things due to both poverty and religious code. She enjoyed reveling in the picture she could now afford to paint.

"I feel sexy," Parton said. "I like being a woman. If I'd-a been a man, I'd-a probably been a drag queen."

Two questions later, after a lighthearted reference to *Best Little Whorehouse* and rounds of laughter, a female journalist solemnly asked for Parton's opinion on sex work. The crowd of reporters gasped, apparently sensing something accusatory about the question or its timing. Parton's smile fell a little, and she took a second to gather her response.

"Oh, I close the whorehouse down," Parton said to laughs before turning serious. "I love everybody. . . . And, like I say, who am I to judge? I got enough problems of my own." Parton paused for a beat, but the room remained silent. She turned back to the questioner, as if to make sure she would have to squirm, too. "Are you a prostitute?" The woman looked down, embarrassed.

For Parton, the old boys came in many forms: Hollywood directors, Nashville producers, media interviewers. As shown by the female journalist in the UK, though, Parton's exchanges with women were often just as problematic.

In 1977 on *The Barbara Walters Special*, Walters caught up with Parton playing a rodeo in Kansas City—the sort of gig her considerable stardom had not quite yet outgrown. Walters interviewed Parton, then thirty-one and beginning her pop music crossover, on the tour bus she shared with her band. Over the course of the conversation, Walters asked her if any "hanky panky" went on amid Parton and her band; whether she hit puberty at a young age; whether her breasts were real; why she wore the tacky wigs and makeup; how she could possibly keep a husband from straying if she was always on the road. (Parton: "I've got better things to do than to sit around in my room thinkin', 'Oh, what's Carl doin' tonight?'")

At one point, Walters asked Parton to stand up.

"I want people to see—you know," Walters said as she drew an hourglass with her hands.

"I'm not all that curvy in this outfit," Parton said as she stood up to oblige.

"Oh, it's not bad," Walters said, looking over at the camera crew to make sure they were getting the shot while Parton put her hands on her hips and endured the stunt. "Do you give your measurements?"

"No," Parton said. "I always just say I weigh a hundred and twenty."

Eventually Parton felt compelled to point out that she was a human being.

"I'm very real where it counts . . . and that's inside—as far as my outlook on life and the way I care about people and the way I care about myself," Parton said. "Show business is a moneymaking joke."

"But do you ever feel that you're a joke," Walters said, her cadence making a statement rather than a question. "That people make fun of you."

"Oh, I know they make fun of me," Parton said. "All these years people has [sic] thought the joke was on me, but it's actually been on the public. I know exactly what I'm doing, and I can change it anytime."

Parton went on to explain that her deep security—in her talent, in her good heart, in all the things Walters didn't ask her about—was precisely why she could "piddle around" with makeup and clothes in a manner in which she, not society and its would-be approval, was in command.

That the 1977 interview is disturbing in hindsight suggests that women have come far, at least in the matter of media treatment. While women still get sexist questions, most of today's leading talk-show hosts wouldn't treat Parton with such plain disrespect, and if they did, an army of pissed-off Twitter users would be hot on their heels.

Even sympathetic interviewers such as Oprah Winfrey, with whom Parton had an obvious mutual affection and respect, fixated on Parton's body. On her talk show in the late eighties, Winfrey—herself no stranger to unrelenting attention about her physique—had Parton stand up for the audience to examine her not once but twice.

Phil Donahue added a male perspective to the sexist interview gantlet.

"I know guys who wouldn't let you out of the house," Donahue told Parton on his hit talk show in the mid-eighties. Parton laughed and assured him that her husband wasn't possessive. An audience member then wanted to know whether

her husband had helped her in her career. He preferred to stay out of her business affairs and its show business trappings, Parton explained.

"That's hard to believe he could be so removed from your professional life," Donahue replied.

Parton offered a thoughtful response, and suddenly Donahue was next to the stage reaching his hand toward her. He had stopped listening and was on to the next thing—you guessed it.

"You won't mind if I ask you to just stand up for just one second," Donahue said, ushering her up onto her feet.

Donahue and Winfrey both asked Parton to address her childlessness. By then she was past the age of forty, the question having shifted from "will you" to "why didn't you."

"That's by choice, isn't it?" Donahue asked.

"No, actually I can't have children," Parton replied, offering the same line she gave Winfrey about "female problems." The truth, Parton has admitted in recent years, was more complicated; prior to her partial hysterectomy she had imagined having children but instead focused on her career— a preference so unacceptable for a woman of child-bearing age at the time that she sometimes circled around it when answering the question over the years.

These interview time capsules, which perhaps say more about the cultural moment than they do about the interviewers, amount to a thorough compilation of all the questions successful women—from celebrities to politicians to any woman with a career in the public eye—receive while men don't.

Socioeconomic class is another matter, even slower than race or gender to arise in the American consciousness. On her television special, Walters asked about Parton's childhood, and Parton offered an earnest answer about the log cabin, the Little Pigeon River, the many children. Walters then interjected with a tone that I recognize well: the upper-middle-class or affluent woman diminishing a "poor" woman's origins.

"Dolly, where I come from, would I have called you a hillbilly?"

Parton smiled. "If you had of, it would have been something very natural, but I would have probably kicked your shins or something." Parton laughed, Walters didn't.

"But when I think of hillbillies, am I thinking of your kind of people?" Walters continued.

On television, Parton at least had the opportunity to respond in real time and hope the producers would edit the tape in a fair manner. Print was a much more dicey prospect: chatting with a writer, most often a man, for him to go off and write what he pleased.

In one particularly barf-worthy *Rolling Stone* story, penned in 1977 by Chet Flippo, the longtime preeminent country music writer, Flippo unfurls a middle-aged man's conquest fantasy about the time he spent with Parton for the story. She rides next to him in a convertible, him imagining the encounter as a date—he should have made dinner reservations, he told her. He was sure to reference that a couple conversations took place in her hotel room, though that was standard protocol for stars doing press on the road. He ended on a quote about Parton newly sprouting breasts as a child and the other children tearing at her jacket to see underneath, and by then a reader wonders whether he's just making shit up. Magazine journalists at the time weren't known for their meticulous notes, and in this case the gonzo male-writer adventure was at Parton's expense.

What do you do if you're Dolly Parton and subjected to these absurd sorts of celebrity interviews for decades? You take a movie role that allows you to play the media member. In the 1992 romantic comedy *Straight Talk*, Parton is a small-town woman who leaves her deadbeat boyfriend to find a new life in Chicago. She ends up as a radio talk-show "psychologist" forced to hide her working-class background and lack of college degree.

Parton noted in her autobiography that, unlike some of her film experiences, she loved making *Straight Talk*, in large part because director Barnet Kellman "was willing to share what he knew with me" and "had a nice way of doing it." Her natural wit was allowed to shine, her own countryisms often making it into the script, which finds her at odds with (and falling for) a wily newspaper reporter. Just as she had previously set a male boss straight in *9 to 5*, reclaimed the joke about her breasts, and turned the word "Hollywood" into "Dollywood," with *Straight Talk* she took control—and put herself in the interviewer's chair.

THE FREEDOM TO WORK

Parton started the 1980s with her first movie role, Doralee in *9 to 5*, and ended the decade with what might be her most beloved one: Truvy, the sweet-and-sassy beauty shop owner in 1989's *Steel Magnolias*.

She recalled in her autobiography that director Herbert Ross "didn't particularly like me or Julia Roberts at the start and [he] was very hard on her. . . . He told me I couldn't act." A generation of women would disagree. At a spring 2017 screening of the quintessential tearjerker in Austin, tickets came with tiny faux hairspray bottles that Alamo Drafthouse theater employees had labeled "Truvy's." The mostly female audience cheered when the character came on-screen.

Earlier this year, in a *Garden & Gun* spread reflecting on

the film, co-star Shirley MacLaine remembered Parton as a heroically easygoing presence in spite of stresses on set.

"It was really hot," MacLaine said. "There was Dolly with a waist cincher no more than sixteen inches around and heels about two feet high and a wig that must have weighed twenty-three pounds. And she's the only one who didn't sweat. She never complained about anything. Never. The rest of us were always complaining."

Screenwriter Robert Harling remembered Parton the same way.

"We were shooting part of the Christmas scene, and this was in the dead of August, and we were sitting out on the porch of Truvy's beauty shop," Harling said. "We were waiting, and there was a lot of stop and start. The women were dressed for Christmas, and Dolly was sitting on the swing. She had on that white cashmere sweater with the marabou around the neck, and she was just swinging, cool as a cucumber. Julia said, 'Dolly, we're dying and you never say a word. Why don't you let loose?' Dolly very serenely smiled and said, 'When I was young and had nothing, I wanted to be rich and famous, and now I am. So I'm not going to complain about anything.'"

Maybe that's why she isn't known to complain about the mistreatments I've outlined here. Parton makes a critique in her way, though. When *Cineaste* magazine asked her in 1990 what she'd discovered in making *Steel Magnolias*, Parton didn't say "that male bosses are still assholes ten years after *9 to 5.*" She instead defended one of her castmates from sexism by letting herself stand in for the perpetrator.

"Daryl Hannah was the big surprise to me. She's beautiful and sweet as anything, but lord, what an actress," Parton said. ". . . I had no idea what a great talent that girl had, 'cause I'd always thought of her as the pretty, long-legged blonde, y'know, getting my head into the same kind of stereotyped thinkin' that annoys me when it happens to me. Daryl takes her acting very seriously and has a curious intelligence and intuition about her. Rare."

In this way, Parton was a skillful, "uneducated" ambassador of a movement attributed to college campuses and activist circles. Most women I grew up among in rural Kansas do not know who Gloria Steinem is, but they know the lines in Parton's late twentieth-century movies by heart and recognize themselves in her image.

Steinem wrote books about reproductive rights, the patriarchal institution of marriage, and the socioeconomic inequality that often accompanies motherhood. Parton gave *Maclean's* the same message in 2014: "One of the reasons I think I've done so well is because I've had the freedom to work," Parton said. "I never had children and I never had a husband who's wanted to bitch about everything I did."

In one of the more improbable photographs from my

childhood, a yellowed square developed around 1984, I'm about four years old and wearing a white tank top printed with the *Ms.* magazine logo. The tiny kids' shirt must have been bought at a garage sale; no one in my family subscribed to *Ms.*, and I'd never even heard of Gloria Steinem's seminal periodical until I was a college-educated adult. But there I am, in rural Kansas in the 1980s, wearing a piece of feminist apparel—not because my mom wanted to make a statement, I assume, but because it was on the five cents table in someone's Wichita driveway.

I tweeted the photo just before seeing Steinem speak a few weeks prior to the 2016 presidential election: "Seeing @GloriaSteinem tonight! No feminism talk in 1980s rural KS, but Mom embodied it—& got me this at a yard sale." Whoever runs Steinem's account "liked" my tweet, which I noted was one of her mere fifteen or so such "likes" at the time—that small, silly transference perhaps my most treasured encounter with a hero.

To have Steinem or even someone representing her on social media appreciate a short bit about my mother—raised in abuse and poverty, seventeen when she became pregnant with me, tenacious as a worker paying the bills, intellectually and creatively gifted but without the chance to go to college, coveted as a woman deemed beautiful—somehow took my bifurcated socioeconomic experience and made it whole.

That evening at Steinem's talk on the University of Texas campus, I was struck by her explanation for how such venomous misogyny could overrun the presidential election in 2016. The moment a woman is statistically most likely to be murdered by her male abuser, Steinem pointed out, is when she escapes. Losing control of her is the unbearable threat that makes the violent ex-husband snap.

Expanding this idea to a patriarchy losing control of half of the U.S. population would indeed explain a lot about recent years: Abortion provider George Tiller's murder in Wichita in 2009, Hillary Clinton's treatment and loss in 2016, the reliable track record of violence against and hatred toward women among male perpetrators of this century's mass-shooting epidemic. It would explain, too, perhaps, how a self-possessed, powerful woman like Parton gets turned into a boob joke.

Like Steinem, Parton is an icon of American womanhood in the twentieth century, still going full force today, perhaps with the energy other women their age who made more orthodox decisions must offer to their grandchildren. Steinem did not come from wealth, but the two women nonetheless had different experiences of socioeconomic class: one went to college, and one took a guitar to Nashville. In different ways and with different tacks, they both charted the course for us to nominate a woman for president in 2016.

When a woman eventually does become president, she will face the same sexist media questions that women like Dolly Parton, Gloria Steinem, and Hillary Clinton have faced, and she will be criticized for her appearance and decisions as all of them have been. She will remember when men held some sort of power she was forced to navigate, whether the harassment Doralee survived for a paycheck, the body-shaming Parton received in Hollywood, or the second-guessing she received from accountants on her own payroll. But she will be this country's first female boss, her leadership inevitably shaped by the trials of womanhood.

In *9 to 5*, while their boss is collared and chained in his own bedroom, the triumphant female employees restructure the entire office with a spree of overdue raises, recognition for cubicles full of women, and some productivity-enhancing redecorating to boot.

So that some female might have such a chance to similarly restructure this ailing democracy, we must give women the freedom to do feminism however they please, whether it strikes us as correct or not. Women dismissing female supporters of Democratic socialist Bernie Sanders, when he opposed Clinton in the 2016 primaries, is not all that different from Barbara Walters criticizing Parton's style choices in 1977.

If Parton's struggles and successes as an implicit rather

than explicit feminist teach us anything, it's that the most authentic female power does not always align with the politics of a movement. If you take Parton's decisions thirty years ago and hold them up against some of the things said and written by activists, academics, and other movement-approved experts from the same time, I would wager that Parton's feminism has aged just as well and in some cases far better.

Lucky for all of us, there is a generation of women coming into power that benefited from both, whether directly or indirectly. They didn't all get to go to college, but they are all the daughters of *9 to 5*—the children against whose lives one can map Parton's metamorphosis from country star to business empress to global icon. They are old enough to be divorced but young enough to still get asked whether they'll finally have a baby; old enough to remember record players in every house but young enough to have been shaped by hip-hop. They watched their mothers be patronized and mistreated so that some future generation might not have to be, and they are equipped to undo the gains made by anti-feminist backlashes over the course of their lifetimes. Today, they are the three women fed up at the office, ready to join forces and hog-tie the male boss until they get some goddamn respect.

Some people might describe *9 to 5* as a revenge fantasy,

but I think of it as a parable about justice. It isn't their boss's suffering they want but their own fair treatment—a request that could be misconstrued as misandry only in the eyes of male privilege.

During Parton's hugely successful 2016 tour for her album *Pure and Simple*, between song performances, she offered a running commentary to make sure everyone knew who was cutting the checks. She objectified the hot male cowboy who brought out her instruments: "He's handsome, ain't he, girls? He's purdy, ain't he, boys? . . . You know that old saying: Make yourself useful and ornamental."

The fired drummer, she explained to the audience, had frowned at her costumes for the show. It was supposed to be a simple, stripped-down production evoking a front porch in Tennessee rather than a Vegas mega-show, and here was Dolly with her usual rhinestones and big hair and heels. She should make her wardrobe more plain, too, he told her.

By now a master at deciding what the public gets to know, Parton has a way of being careful with details. But this story—of a male employee giving Parton advice about her stage appearance, when she's been successfully steering her own music productions for decades—sounded exact, and she clearly relished sharing a tale about being the boss.

She surely remembers when she wasn't. In her book *Dolly*, she included a black-and-white photo of Wagoner ceremoniously presenting her twenty-something self with a piece of precious jewelry; young Parton wears a beehive wig and a tight, dutiful smile. The caption reads "Me and Porter: Oh boy, a ring, but what I wanted was a raise."

In the end, Parton didn't just get a raise—she got the whole world, and the drummer she employed for this tour apparently hadn't heard. She told him the two words every woman should at least have the chance to say: "You're fired."

"I left him in Nashville. I saved a lot of money," Parton said, gesturing affectionately toward the drum machine in his place. "And it don't talk back."

PART FOUR

DOLLY PARTON CEMENTS
HER ICON STATUS

— WINTER 2017—

During the 2017 Emmy Awards, Dolly Parton reunited with *9 to 5* co-stars Jane Fonda and Lily Tomlin to present an award. All three were nominated for Emmys themselves: Fonda and Tomlin for acting in the Netflix comedy series *Grace and Frankie*, in which they play upper-class friends in Southern California, and Parton for producing the 2016 television movie *Christmas of Many Colors*, in which she plays an Appalachian sex worker.

Onstage with Parton and Tomlin, Fonda pointed out their role as feminist elders.

"Back in 1980, in [*9 to 5*], we refused to be controlled by a sexist, egotistical, lying, hypocritical bigot," Fonda said.

Tomlin added, to cheers, making an obvious reference to the sitting president, "In 2017, we still refuse to be controlled by a sexist, hypocritical, lying, egotistical bigot."

For her part, Parton cracked a joke, referencing a season-two story line from their series: "I'm just hoping that I'm going to get one of those *Grace and Frankie* vibrators in my swag bag tonight."

Hers was the least directly political comment of the three. It was also the one most assured to vex a man like Donald Trump—in whose eyes women exist for his pleasure, diminish in value as they age, and need a man to achieve sexual pleasure. What's more anti-Trump than a rich seventy-one-year-old woman fantasizing about a sex toy on national television after his name was invoked?

The stars of that feminist film found themselves addressing the past in the present, their fictional office boss made leader of the actual world.

Like the entire nation, for which conservatism now shapes law and dominates the White House, the country music industry is suffering a swing backward, against gains women made in the late twentieth century. During the first half of 2016, songs sung by female artists accounted for less than 10 percent of country radio plays, according to *Forbes* magazine. In that same time, only five female artists appeared on *Billboard*'s Top 30 Country Airplay charts.

The previous year, an influential country-radio consultant, Keith Hill, explained why stations keep their rotations overwhelmingly male. Hill told *Country Aircheck*, "If you want to make ratings in country radio, take females out." Women, he said, were "just not the lettuce in our salad. The lettuce is

Luke Bryan, Blake Shelton, Keith Urban, and artists like that. The tomatoes of our salad are the females."

The comment sparked an overdue controversy about an old problem, and female artists expressed their displeasure. Martina McBride sold "tomato" shirts to raise money for her charity. Jennifer Nettles tweeted that the moment was a "big old vagina-shaped opportunity."

Men and women alike on music's business side defended Hill's comment with claims about numbers and data: There aren't enough good female records, female songs don't test as well, even female listeners prefer male singers when you crunch the numbers. But it wasn't always so. Whatever factors are behind such data, they say more about prevailing cultural attitudes of the moment than about the quality of women's music.

The last time Dolly Parton had a solo number-one hit, "Why'd You Come in Here Looking Like That" in 1989, female artists were riding high in the industry, making way for the halcyon 1990s of Reba, Faith, and Shania. But a recent Stanford University study found that, despite record labels continuing to introduce new female artists, women have fallen down the charts since the turn of the millennium.

Parton has attributed her own absence from the charts to the fact that she is now an artist of a certain age. "When the new country came along, any artist over thirty-five was thought to be a has-been," she told *Rolling Stone* in 2003. "And, Lord, I've been around for so long that people looked at me like a legend. But I wasn't near done. I felt like I was better than I ever was. I feel like I'm just now seasoned enough to know how to be in this business. And I thought, 'Well, hell, I'm not going down with the rest of them old farts. I'm gonna find some new ways of doing it.' And that's exactly what I did."

Parton had founded her own record label in 1994, at age forty-eight, as pop sounds were dominating the country-music industry. "I thought, 'Well, now I can record the stuff I really want to,' and I don't have fourteen managers and record executives saying, 'Oh, you gotta be more commercial, you gotta be more pop,'" she told *Rolling Stone*. "I thought, 'I don't care if I write [a song that is] six or seven minutes long—I'm gonna tell the story.' I'm not gonna think, 'Oh, I have to cut this down to fit the radio.' If they play it on the radio, fine. Doubt if they would, and don't care anymore."

Today's young female singer-songwriters who follow in Parton's footsteps—old twang, modern ideas, gothic country themes, spiritual vulnerability—get good reviews, sell records, and sell out shows whether they're underplayed on country radio or not. But such artists—from superstar Miranda Lambert to rising sensation Kacey Musgraves to indie favorite Valerie June—are working in an industry currently betting against them.

KEEPING IT REAL

Parton's late-career decisions have revealed a commitment to authenticity over hit-making. Since going rogue with her own label in the early nineties, Parton has put out more than a dozen solo albums of new material. Some of it—released just as slick pop country acts like Keith Urban and Rascal Flatts were taking over the airwaves—is thoroughly bluegrass, including a 2001 cover of Collective Soul's rock hit "Shine" that won her a Grammy.

The music from the first half of her career, though, remains her signature and is now being discovered by a generation born after Parton disappeared from country radio. To them, it seems, she is not just an entertainer but a spiritual godmother, her big-haired 1970s likeness on devotional candles in trendy stores and online shopping carts. A phrase that a friend of mine recently applied to a beloved public radio host seems apt to describe Dolly's role today: "one of the few living astral moms."

Whether Parton has another groundbreaking hit or not, her entire life is now understood to have broken ground—for female artists, for poor girls with dreams, for women who would like to be bosses without hiding their breasts. This late awakening to Parton was a gradual unfolding, but its tipping point might have been England's Glastonbury Festival in 2014.

After having no manager for seventeen years, in the early 2000s Parton hired Nashville manager Danny Nozell to help organize a tour. Nozell crafted a plan to market her work to young people around the world. She sold out a tour in Europe in 2007, an arena tour in 2008, and two Australian tours. But Parton said no to booking requests from Glastonbury—an immense, decidedly rock-and-roll gathering—from 2006 to 2013. Her fervent fan base has been global for decades, but she worried the festival wouldn't be a good fit, according to a 2014 interview with the *Guardian.*

When she finally took the leap in 2014 as a Glastonbury headliner, not even Parton understood what was about to happen: An estimated 180,000 people gathered to see her—the biggest crowd in festival history, surpassing numbers for a Rolling Stones performance. Another 2.6 million watched live on the BBC, the network's largest-ever audience for its festival coverage.

Glastonbury was a long way from the East Tennessee farm where, as a child, Parton made a mock microphone from a tin can and sang for the hogs. She had left that farm fifty years prior but honored those origins for the huge international crowd with a song called "Mud," penned for the infamously muddy festival. "I grew up on a farm," Parton said, "so this mud ain't nothin' new to me."

Part of Parton's successful strategy for connecting with new fans in recent years has been to collaborate with much younger artists. On pop star Kesha's most recent album, out last August, Parton sings a duet of her own number-one hit from 1980, "Old Flames (Can't Hold a Candle to You)," which Kesha's mother, Pebe Sebert, wrote. Earlier this year, Parton covered Brandi Carlile's "The Story," for an album benefiting a nonprofit that aids refugee children. She won a 2017 Grammy for Best Country Duo/Group Performance for her "Jolene" recording remixed by young a cappella group Pentatonix.

Parton has long shown up for her millennial goddaughter, Miley Cyrus—making a cameo on her Disney TV show, bringing her onstage, singing with her on *The Voice*—perhaps to the benefit of both. A journalist friend of mine once told me that he had been watching the World Cup at a bar in Venezuela with Hugo Chávez when Chávez's daughter told him that she and her friend loved the "new Miley Cyrus song" about a woman named Jolene. He showed them a video of the Parton original on his phone, and they were dazzled.

Much of the new fandom might not be able to name more than five Parton songs, but Parton's presence is so multifaceted that they will have plenty of opportunity to learn more. Her songs have been recorded by such wide-ranging superstars as Patti Smith and Kitty Wells. Some of her movies, most notably *9 to 5* and *Steel Magnolias*, are now considered classics. But late-career Parton is much more—a philanthropic force and an auspiciously progressive voice in conservative spaces.

Her literacy project, Imagination Library, has given more than 80 million books to over one million children around the world, according to the foundation.

Her outspoken progressivism regarding gay and transgender rights, gender parity, and other issues have pushed country music to evolve, while her open Christian faith and homespun vernacular have made her a bridge between crossover fans and the poor, rural South.

During the fall 2017 semester, the University of Tennessee offered a history course that used Parton's life story to examine Appalachia in the twentieth century, from child-labor laws to today's economic struggles. There is a rose named after her; there is a film, the 2015 indie *Seeking Dolly Parton*, named after the rose. Parton is now to country music what Oprah Winfrey is to media—a natural talent who, simply by being herself, transcended an industry to transform society.

Part of the transformation she helmed was women's progress in country music; Nashville is still rooted in patriarchy but has certainly progressed since she showed up in the 1960s.

Perhaps due to her looks and persona, though, until recent years Parton had not been treated by music journalists or Hollywood with the gravitas long ago afforded, say, Loretta Lynn, whose life was mined for the Oscar-winning biopic *Coal Miner's Daughter* and whose music spurred the admiration and collaboration of indie darling Jack White.

But seen in the light of the twenty-first century, with woke young fans and greater female representation in the media that sets the narratives about her, Parton's place in culture finally shifts from objectified female body to the divine feminine—a sassy priestess in high heels.

GIVING BACK

Parton has said that one of her greatest professional joys is her relationship to children who receive free books in the mail each month, from birth until age five, through Imagination Library, which she founded in 1995. Innocent of her celebrity, those kids call her "the book lady," she told *PBS NewsHour* in 2013. Parton released her first children's album this fall.

"Children have always responded to me because I have that cartoon-character look," Parton told *Time* magazine in 2009, when she released her own children's book titled *I Am a Rainbow*. "I'm overexaggerated and my voice is small and my name is Dolly and I'm kind of like a Mother Goose character."

Her father Lee's illiteracy inspired her concern for reading. That family background, the cause for Parton's famous climb from poverty, might be why the first book each child in the program receives is *The Little Engine That Could*—the hard-work-and-gumption lessons of which are vintage Dolly. The story has been performed as a live show at Dollywood's Imagination Playhouse, which brings many of the program's selections to life.

Imagination Library, often facilitated by local libraries, requires no income documentation or other hoop-jumping— just a quick form with an address and the child's birth date to confirm age eligibility. This decision by the umbrella Dollywood Foundation indicates someone involved knows what it's like to be a child in need. Since everyone is eligible, the neediest children can benefit without feeling ashamed of being recipients of a poor-people's program.

Parton's relief funds for victims of last year's Smoky Mountain wildfires were similarly low on red tape. Affected families, whether homeowners or renters, simply provided proof of address to receive $1,000 per month for six months from the Dollywood Foundation, with few questions asked. At the end of that period, last May, Parton visited some of the nine hundred families who had received assistance to make an announcement, and the *Tennessean* shared video of an exchange with one beneficiary.

"I'm gonna give you an additional five thousand dollars," Parton said, making the total gift $11,000 for each household.

"An additional—" an older man in a University of Tennessee ball cap said.

"That's like a bonus that you didn't know you were gettin'," Parton said, slapping him on the shoulder.

"God bless you for doin' this for us," he said in a serious tone. "For all these people."

"It's the least I can do," Parton said. "I'm a Smoky Mountain girl. I mean, this is home. Charity begins at home, right?"

A white-haired woman sitting next to the man interjected. "Nobody but you would be so kind and generous," she said, starting to cry. Parton, standing, wiped tears from the woman's face.

"I'm sure nearly anybody up here would do that," Parton said. "These are good people."

"You're our people," the man replied, nodding. "Whether we're your people or not, you're our people."

"You *are* my people," Parton said.

To address the long-term needs of those who lost their homes and more, she gave $3 million to establish the Mountain Tough fund, through which social workers can secure medication for fire-related health problems, rides to work, and more for low-income fire victims.

I have observed surprised reactions to Parton's philanthropy, from the millions of books mailed to children to the millions of dollars raised for fire victims, from the decades of high school scholarships to Tennessee high school seniors to the health care foundation she established in 1983 and named for the country doctor who delivered her. Other famous people are as generous as she is, one imagines. But I've never seen people so taken aback upon learning about celebrity philanthropy as those who learn about Parton's.

Perhaps this is because, for most of her giving over the years, there has been no photo op or press release—just a quiet check and Parton's name on a board of directors. Imagination Library, in particular, kept a low profile for nearly thirty years, which must have been Parton's preference at the time. But children's author Robert Munsch, featured in a 2009 documentary about the book program, got down to the real matter of why her good heart comes as such a revelation.

"I thought of Dolly Parton as this singer with the really

big boobs who was in the movies with, like, the really big boobs," Munsch said. "I didn't really have much of an idea."

BIG BUSINESS

People might not have much of an idea about the extent of Parton's business empire, either. In addition to her music, books, movies, TV shows, and even restaurant forays over the years, in 1986 she co-founded Sandollar Productions with her manager Sandy Gallin. The company's successes range from blockbuster hits like the 1991 comedy *Father of the Bride* and the television series *Buffy the Vampire Slayer* to cultural milestones like *Stories from the Quilt*, the 1989 AIDS film that won the Academy Award for best documentary.

Surpassing even blockbuster Hollywood success, in financial terms, is Parton's enduring Dollywood amusement park in Pigeon Forge.

Writer Keith Bellows, who lived in East Tennessee for fifteen years, vouched for the attraction's deep connection to the local people in a story for *National Geographic Traveler* in 2009.

"I was charmed by [Dolly's] practice of populating the park with genuine Appalachian craftspeople, musicians, artists," Bellows wrote. "That was rare back then—but she's always been a trendsetter."

Parton told Bellows that decision was foundational to the business: "I wanted people working there who were connected with the land and the local culture. They made it real, not phony. It made me feel comfortable. And I guess I thought it would make the visitors feel that way, too."

The place was previously a Silver Dollar City location, modeled on a park in Branson, Missouri, with a rural Ozarks theme. Since Parton transformed the park in 1986, her presence is everywhere, including a Dolly museum and a replica of the house she grew up in.

While many amusement parks create an atmosphere of fantasy intended to sweep visitors into another place full of magical characters, Parton's impulse was to highlight the natural setting and working people that shaped her—keeping it local before local was cool. "I'm keen to maintain the soul of the place," Parton told Bellows. "To celebrate God's beauty—that means go for a nice walk, smell that air, feel the temperature, hold on to the sense of the moment, take a drift on a trail, look deeply into the stream. That means so much more than all the artifice in the world."

Country music scholar Pamela Fox, examining country music autobiographies in the academic journal *American Quarterly* in 1998, pointed out that Dollywood not only celebrates the Smoky Mountains for the rest of the world, but champions that region's poorest people within the context of their own home. "Chiding those critics who dismiss the theme park as a vanity project," Fox wrote, "Parton insists that the business honors 'her people' by employing 'mostly real hillbillies' to showcase mountain culture. At the same time, she planned the park to resemble old-time, small-town carnivals—the ostensible Other of that hardscrabble world."

A cynic might say that, even with good intentions, Parton has exploited that socioeconomic, geographic Other—the rural poor—for her own gain. By employing people of the region, one could argue that Dollywood demands those people make a performance of their authentic lives, as other cultures and entire races have been commanded to do for more privileged people in exchange for money and survival. But the difference with Dollywood is that Parton was and is of the place.

Parton sometimes jokes about being "white trash," a term I refuse to use as a white person who grew up in rural poverty but one that she earned the right to reclaim. Directly oppose degradation or seize its means—two valid approaches, the latter being Parton's preferred method. To fight the dehumanization of the rural poor, she got rich, went home, and turned Appalachia into a performance before rich, urban developers could. It's not unlike her habit of cracking a joke about her breasts before a male talk-show host has the chance to.

Located just a few miles from the spot where she was born,

Dollywood demonstrates Parton's loyalty to her people, not just in the past they share but in the present moment. She cuts their checks, sends their high schoolers to college, funds a foundation to ensure their health care, and holds a telethon when wildfires take their houses. While wages at the amusement park are standard for that industry—low hourly pay for seasonal hires such as students on summer break—all employees have access to an onsite health care center, and full-time employees of the park receive comprehensive health insurance benefits.

Make no mistake, Parton set out to get rich and enjoy being rich, and that she has done. This year, for the first time, thanks to Dollywood's continued boom and her 2016 tour, she made the *Forbes* list of the world's one hundred highest-paid entertainers—at number seventy-one, above Rihanna, Billy Joel, and Katy Perry.

Her wealth hasn't changed her tastes, according to her. Parton has said that she and her husband enjoy hitting the road in an RV and getting their meals from fast-food drive-through windows.

"I'm a truck stop girl," she said in the *National Geographic Traveler* story. "Honest. I'm not an act. I go into Cracker Barrel and browse the shelf. Mostly I look for real stuff. My husband and I pull off the road to look at any old antique store. It's 'Dolly is coming'—I blow in there, fly into the room, and get something wonderful that says I've been there. I just love my junk stuff. Wigs are what people think of when they picture me. But what I really look for is what my Daddy would love."

She also has a taste for real estate, she told *Billboard* in 2014. "It's not to say, 'Hey, look at me,'" she explained. "I'd rather buy property than play the stock market." She owns a residence in Los Angeles and two in Tennessee. (One imagines there might be more she doesn't divulge publicly.)

That much of her real estate is located in her home state parallels every other aspect of her career. She could afford to look refined and sophisticated but has held fast to a personal style modeled after her poor-country vision of glamour. She could adapt the way she speaks in the company of higher classes but keeps on saying "ain't." She could sing and speak about her world travels and decades of rarefied experiences but keeps talking about the poor folks what brung her. As Jancee Dunn wrote for *Rolling Stone* in 2003, "Many people who are raised in near-poverty try to distance themselves from their upbringing, but not Parton, whose ticket out turned into a round-trip."

That round-trip is not just in spirit but in the flesh. Parton is known to be physically present at the park, whether for an event or to shop in her own stores. "I love Dollywood, because I love to go shopping up there in the stores," she told

Dunn. "I think, 'Oh, good, I don't have to pay for this.' I'm taking advantage of myself."

HITS AND MISSES

However thoughtful and self-aware, Parton's career and empire is not impeccable. One truly problematic rhinestone in Parton's business crown is Dixie Stampede, a dinner-theater experience that will celebrate its thirtieth year in 2018.

Held in a 35,000-square-foot rodeo arena that seats more than a thousand people, the daily show features horse-riding stunts like barrel racing and musical productions while visitors eat chicken with their fingers. While Parton's message is usually a class-conscious argument for love and acceptance, Dixie Stampede is a squarely patriotic event with a heavy dose of white-washed nostalgia for the Antebellum South. The show's overarching theme is the Civil War; patrons are asked to choose which side they'll cheer for.

Locations include Pigeon Forge, home of Dollywood and her nearby water park, and a second spot in Branson, Missouri. Another operated for eighteen years in Myrtle Beach, South Carolina, until Parton spent $11 million to transform it into a pirate-themed dinner-theater attraction in 2010. A shorter-lived location opened near Disney World in Florida in 2003 and closed five years later.

In 2015, the remaining Tennessee and Missouri locations underwent a $2.5 million update, including new music and special effects. According to Parton's website, by that point more than 20 million people had visited.

I went to the Branson location with my family years before that update and found the operation to be far removed from Parton in both spirit and actual presence. A recording of Parton's voice came from speakers multiple times during the show, suggesting that she herself might appear, which I found maddening and insulting to visitors' intelligence.

As for the show itself, I grew up going to rodeos and once loved a good barrel race as much as the next gal. But when I waited in line at Dixie Stampede, I was in college, learning about my home state of Kansas's pivotal role in sparking the Civil War by declaring itself a free state. During that period, much blood was shed at slave-holding Missouri's border; Kansas has a strained relationship with Missouri and Confederacy glorification to this day. Perhaps that is why, even as a relatively ignorant and privilege-oblivious young white woman, I wasn't impressed with a story line that sanitized the Civil War as cheesy entertainment.

Last August, after the renovation, *Slate* culture writer Aisha Harris penned an overdue critique of Dixie Stampede, calling it a "lily-white kitsch extravaganza that play-acts the Civil War but never once mentions slavery." The Confederate flag doesn't make an appearance to represent the South, but a gray flag evokes that army's uniform color. The show ultimately wraps with a message that we're all part of one United States of America.

Attending two 2017 performances to research her piece, Harris noted surprise at the number of people of color among the crowd and employees. But she found the production a troubling, delusional spectacle.

"Standing in front of the box office were two young women who looked like the cast of *The Beguiled*, or Southern belles from *Gone with the Wind*, greeting patrons as they made their way into the building," Harris wrote. "Once inside and past the ticket scanners, you were forced to take a group photo in one of several partitioned quarters in front of a green backdrop. Rather than immortalizing this unwanted re-enactment in the form of a $30 souvenir, I asked not to have my picture taken and hurried past while trying to blend in with the family in front of me."

Harris, who shared that she was a Parton fan, pointed out that this unfortunate piece of Parton's portfolio exemplified the denial that allows white people to defend Confederate monuments or to see white-supremacist rallies and anti-racism protests as moral equivalents.

"Even though the South is built upon the foundation of slavery, a campy show produced by a well-meaning country superstar can make believe it's not," Harris wrote.

A few weeks after her story ran, Harris reported for *Slate* that she had reached out for a response from Dixie Stampede and been told via email that they would "evaluate" her piece.

While that initial response could be described as lacking, Harris generously shared, in a *Slate* follow-up, her hope that the business might make real changes. "As an admirer of Parton's other work in movies and music," she wrote, "and as someone who believes that it matters how honestly we tell our nation's history, it's nice to hear that my review might inspire the show's creators to reconsider its framing and presentation."

This insensitive portrayal of brutal history is particularly disappointing when one considers that, over the decades, Parton has taken bold stands for the LGBTQ community, for women, and for the poor. Her statement on all the rest, from race to political affiliation, has remained a message of love in general terms. Now, Parton's late-career power and presence happen to coincide with a fractious civic moment. What will she do with it?*

---

* Update: The attraction, now called Dolly Parton's Stampede, has removed references to the Civil War and made other improvements to racial sensitivity. Months after the publication of Harris's critique, the business dropped "Dixie" from its name, a decision Parton explained to *Billboard* in 2020: "When they said 'Dixie' was an offensive word, I thought, 'Well, I don't want to offend anybody. This is a business. We'll just call it The Stampede.' As soon as you realize that [something] is a problem, you should fix it. Don't be a dumbass. That's where my heart is. I would never dream of hurting anybody on purpose."

Onstage during her 2016 tour, Parton at least alluded to that year's divisive presidential election and race-related police shootings and unrest. She referenced the country's volatile state before performing a moving handful of folk songs that were popular the last time our culture was at such a boiling point—the beginning of her career, the fraught 1960s.

Glittering in rhinestones and holding forth with the strong voice from her diaphragm that I've always preferred to the soft, girly voice she affects for some of her hits, she sang "If I Had a Hammer" and other counterculture classics while her unplugged musicians joined her with an upright bass, guitar, and tambourine. Much of the crowd sang along, some through tears.

NIP IT, TUCK IT, SUCK IT

Aging celebrities sometimes confront a moral reckoning. As culture evolves, do their actions and ethics stand the test of time? Bill Cosby's alleged serial rapes* went unchecked amid the sexist culture of his younger days but are the stuff of career ruin today. Meanwhile, sentiment toward Jane Fonda's

---

* "Alleged" was a legally appropriate descriptor when this was first published in 2017. The following year, however, Cosby was convicted on three counts of aggravated indecent assault and sentenced to three to ten years in prison.

Vietnam War protests, for which she was vilified for decades, has softened as prevailing attitudes toward that war became more critical.

For female stars, there is another trial in the maturation process—physical aging. Parton has famously undergone a great deal of plastic surgery and makes no bones about it. She believes she has an image to maintain and seeks to project vitality. "I have done it and will do it again when something in my mirror doesn't look to me like it belongs on Dolly Parton," she wrote in her 1994 autobiography. "I feel it is my duty to myself and my public. My spirit is too beautiful and alive to live in some dilapidated old body if it doesn't have to."

Country music scholar Pamela Fox, in her 1998 *American Quarterly* article, suggested that Parton's impoverished upbringing made her comfortable with a sense of detachment from her own body—previously put to use for farm chores, now for squeezing into a costume.

In the process of surgical reconstruction, Fox wrote, "'Dolly Parton' becomes a separate, almost reified persona which her body literally creates. . . . Parton understands that gender is performance: achieving the right hair color, conforming to a seemingly impossible hourglass bodily ideal. But it is a performance she can pull off with astounding success. . . . She exchanges the class-based objectification of her past for a gender-based one in the present. The Dolly character represents the literal embodiment of her own personal 'dream.'"

Seen in that light, a decision that might cause some feminists to shake their heads turns out to be an honest triumph. In 2004, she told CBS, "I always said, if I see something sagging, bagging, and dragging, I'm going to nip it, tuck it, and suck it. Whatever needs to be done. I mean, it's like I look at myself like a show horse, or a show dog. . . . I've always had nice boobs. I always had a nice body when I was little, but when I lost all that weight, I had them pumped up, and fixed up. They just stand up there like brave little soldiers now. They're real big, they're real expensive, and they're really mine now."

Parton's sense of ownership about her body is a defiant act in a culture that managed to obsess over her breasts so thoroughly that the first cloned mammal, a sheep created from a mammory-gland cell in 1996, was named after her.

Parton's response to double standards about male and female bodies is not to embrace her own aging but, rather, playfully chastise men for theirs. During a 2003 taping of CMT's *Crossroads* series with Melissa Etheridge, Parton told the familiar lore about her song "Jolene"—a pretty bank employee caught her husband's eye early in their marriage, and Parton's song begged her not to take him.

"I look at him now," she joked between songs, next to Etheridge, "[and] I think about hiding his Viagra and saying, 'Go get him.'"

Later in the set, the pair performed another song about jealousy, Etheridge's early-career rock tune "Bring Me Some Water." Parton sang the lyrics with passion and changed the verb "whispering" to something wilder: "Tell me how will I ever be the same / When I know that woman is somewhere screaming your name." As the song wound down, though, Parton's tone changed from tortured to commanding, and with a spoken aside she suddenly invented a younger man for her own amusement. "Hey, little water boy," Parton said, unsmiling, her hand on her hip. "Bring the bucket around." Etheridge cracked up.

During a 2013 *Good Morning America* interview next to Parton, her longtime friend and duet partner Kenny Rogers referred to his own famously altered face and how Parton had chided him for it. "When [the media] got on that whole plastic surgery thing, that was a bit painful even though it was true," Rogers said. "Dolly used to say, 'Look, ol' Kenny's been to Jiffy Suck again.'"

Sitting next to him, Parton took his chin in her hand and examined his face while he tried to pull away. "I think he's really grown into his face-lift now, don't you?" she said and laughed. "He looks great."

Disparate treatment of Parton's and Rogers's respective legacies is less funny.

Parton has written thousands of songs, her cultural impact so profound that in 2005 the National Endowment for the Arts awarded her the country's highest honor for contribution to creative fields, the National Medal of Arts. By contrast, Rogers rose to fame lending his smooth voice to someone else's words.

"I take great pride in not writing hits," Rogers told NPR when his autobiography, *Luck or Something Like It*, was released in 2012. "I write from time to time, but I think great writers have a need to write, and I don't really have that need. I can write if someone sits me down and says, 'Hey let's write a song about this.'"

Plenty of music legends didn't write their own songs, and Rogers's career achievements are immense. But his career benefited from Parton's. As Rogers recalled on *Good Morning America*, he was recording "Islands in the Stream" solo with lackluster results when producer Barry Gibb mused that they needed Parton to "make it pop." Now the song is one of the bestselling duets of all time and a pop-culture mainstay. Parton didn't write that one, but her presence next to him in the studio and onstage is perhaps what ensured his legacy.

"There's no question it's kind of the crown to everything," he added on *GMA*. "To have done the song with her and have it be accepted so highly worldwide. No matter where I go, the one thing they always ask for is 'Islands in the Stream.'"

Despite all this, it was Rogers, not Parton, who became the second recipient of the Country Music Awards' Willie Nelson Lifetime Achievement Award (a year after Nelson himself received it in 2012).

The next year, the award went to Johnny Cash, post-humously. Then, in 2015, when Parton became the first female and fourth performer to receive the award, she suffered the indignity of being cut off when she'd barely begun her acceptance speech.

During the presentation honoring her, *9 to 5* co-star and friend Lily Tomlin spoke before Jennifer Nettles, Pentatonix, Reba McEntire, Kacey Musgraves, Carrie Underwood, and Martina McBride each sang Parton's hits. By the time Parton finally took the stage, one minute into her speech, producers promptly cued her to wrap it up.

"They asked me to hurry it up. They said that they're behind," she told the audience. "But we're talking about a lifetime here." She wrapped up at the two-minute mark with a big smile, saying, "I had a big speech, but they won't let me give it." Then Sharon Stone slowly sauntered across the stage and presented Best Male Artist to Chris Stapleton, who was embarrassed. "If Dolly's still back there," he said, "I'd give her my time." But the show moved on.

The reaction on Twitter from across the cultural and political spectrum was swift.

"Really #CMAawards50 you couldn't let the legendary @DollyParton give her speech for a lifetime of country music? No bueno," film critic Carla Renata tweeted.

Conservative commentator Meghan McCain didn't mince words: "Who in the holy hell wouldn't let @DollyParton finish her speech for her lifetime achievement award?!?!"

And New York drag queen Darienne Lake tweeted, "My biggest devastation of the night, cutting @DollyParton's speech short. Everyone should be fired at the #CMAawards50. EVERYONE!"

Later in the evening, Entertainer of the Year Garth Brooks got plenty of time to speak. I'm not suggesting there was some big conspiracy to cut Parton off and give the time to male performers. But, as the radio programming consultant's "tomato" comment revealed, show business is a world of calculations informed by gender. And that night at the CMAs—if only in a hasty moment subconsciously informed by culture and implicit bias—someone decided that Parton's speech was worth less than a series of moments starring men.

SO MUCH SUBSTANCE

A woman's voice, whether on the radio, onstage, or in a presidential race, will be celebrated but only so far. The airplay will be minimized. The speech will be cut short. Someone will yell, "Lock her up."

Parton, surely among the least divisive figures in pop culture, apparently receives little direct antagonism. But as a female boss, she has faced the sexist onus of "likability." In 2014, *Billboard* asked her, "As a Southern woman, how do you speak your mind and take care of business but remain likable?"

Parton didn't seem to be losing any sleep over the issue. "I'm open and I'm honest," she replied. "I don't dillydally. If there's something going on, I just say it. Sometimes if I get mad, I'll throw out a few cuss words just to prove my point. I've often said I don't lose my temper as much as I use it. I don't do either unless I have to because I love peace and harmony, but when you step in my territory, I will call you on it. People say, 'Oh, you just always seem so happy.' Well, that's the Botox."

The glass ceiling that hindered lifelong public servant Hillary Clinton's campaign battle against a morally bankrupt, incompetent man is the same one that made Dolly Parton answer more questions about her measurements than her songwriting over the decades. The two women took very different paths. But, at almost exactly the same age, they shared an experience—breaking through, toward an equality that they themselves will never enjoy.

Who, then, will follow in Parton's footsteps and reap the benefits of her struggles? While plenty of young artists count Parton as an influence, who could truly take up her mantle?

A couple years ago, VH1 theorized that one such performer might be hip-hop artist Nicki Minaj. Media critic Jade Davis expanded on the theory, citing Minaj's large hair and curves, as well as her business savvy.

"They're also both musicians in lowbrow, male-dominated genres," Davis wrote. "They both embrace being objects in the spaces where they're allowed to exist . . . Parton lovingly refers to herself as the 'backwoods Barbie.' Similarly, Minaj's longest-running and most famous stage [persona] is the Harajuku Barbie. . . . But even though they draw inspiration from the fakest woman on the planet, they keep it realer than anyone. They don't need to stand in front of glowing 'FEMINIST' signs or writhe around with lubricant on their bodies. They live, breathe, and perform what everyone else tries so hard to convey: I own myself."

Indeed, Parton helped pioneer the sort of feminism on display in contemporary pop music: serving up T&A on your own terms, subverting objectification by having a damn good time with it. And she did so while not necessarily sounding like liberal America. On CNN in 2015, a caller asked Parton if she would describe herself as a feminist.

"Oh, I'm a—I'm a female and I believe that everybody should definitely have their rights," she said. "I don't care if you're Black, white, straight, gay, women, men, whatever. I think everybody that has something to offer should be allowed to give it and be paid for it. But, no, I don't consider myself a feminist, not in the term that some people do, because I— I just think we all should be treated with respect."

Her answer might break your heart if, like me, you speak the language of college-educated activists. But I speak another language, too—poor country—and can attest that as an independent teenager in small-town Kansas who believed women and men should receive equal treatment, I might have given a similar answer. So much of what ails our country now, politically, is that we do not share a common set of definitions.

In the context of her native class, Parton's gift to young women is not a statement but an example. One wishes for both from a hero. But, if I could only have one of the two, I'd pick the latter.

Parton's pro-woman example is not lost on today's female

creators. In the 2011 Canadian film *The Year Dolly Parton Was My Mom*, set in rural Winnipeg in the 1970s, a young Parton fan discovers she is adopted. The story is self-aware in its feminist messages.

Hoping to use Parton's music in the film, writer-director Tara Johns managed to get the script to her through a series of contacts just before Parton left on tour. Parton responded with a faxed letter stating that she had spent the weekend reading the script and was over the moon, Johns told women's lifestyle website She Does the City. Parton gave her rights to use nine songs for a small fee, four of which were recorded for the soundtrack by Canadian artists, including Nelly Furtado and the Wailin' Jennys.

"No Canadian film could afford to buy those publishing rights at the going rate," Johns said. Parton even recorded a voiceover for the film. Johns had the idea for the movie after hearing Parton in a radio interview.

"I'd never really listened to Dolly Parton. I mean, the music, yes, but not the woman. Because there were no distractions, no flashy sequins or hair or boobs or whatever, it was just really easy to listen to the substance, and I was blown away by how strong a career woman she was, even way back when," Johns said. "She blazed a trail for so many artists who came after her, and I didn't know that about her. That was a bit of a revelation. I thought it would have been cool when I was eleven or twelve to know that Dolly Parton was a feminist, under all of that."

Johns noted that Parton's pioneering feminism might have been overlooked for the way she went about it. "The whole objectification that most women rail against, she took it, and she went to the wall with it," Johns said. "And in a way, it's a challenge, she sort of challenged that whole concept, that whole way of looking at women. You scrape the very thin veneer of that objectified image and you get so much substance."

Parton's experiments with image are not always so deft. See her 2013 appearance on *The Queen Latifah Show*, soon after Latifah starred in the 2012 remake of *Steel Magnolias*, which featured an all-Black female cast, with Jill Scott playing Parton's iconic beautician character Truvy. In an apparent homage to Latifah, with whom she co-starred in the 2012 movie musical *Joyful Noise*, Parton performed an original rap in a blond afro wig.

"Please welcome one of the baddest rappers in the game, straight out of the 'ville," Latifah said to introduce the segment. "Nashville, that is."

The song had a Grandmaster Flash–style beat and a classic rap theme—don't try to step to this—while telling the story of her life.

Parton started with the classic hip-hop audience

exchange—"Hey, hoooo, hey, hoooo"—and then broke into full East Tennessee: "I'm not callin' nobody names. I'm just sayin' how-*deeee*!"

Parton then pointed out that she and Latifah both have large breasts, but that only one of them is really known for working them. She gestured down at her chest in a skin-tight black leotard with, as ever in recent years, long sleeves (she is rumored to be covered in tattoos).

"Look at dem go!" she rapped about her breasts. "Hey, I'm tweakin. I'm workin'. I'm twerkin'. Hey, Miley—I got your wreckin' balls right *heeya*." Parton added to that last word a breath that is a feature of Southern Protestant dialect. Soon she was singing, "She'll be comin' around the mountain when she comes," over the beat.

The performance, which could have been a producer's idea, is uncomfortable to watch. In inviting Latifah to battle, she referenced belonging to a "redneck mafia," apparently without realizing this might conjure for some viewers the violent and deadly horrors of white supremacy in the South. It seems that Parton's sincere but awkward intention was to tell Latifah's audience that she, too, was an "Other" of sorts, finding her way out of the role society assigned her by performing it.

"You may be the queen," Parton said, "but I am the white-trash princess. Well, me and Honey Boo Boo." Her joke reference to a hit reality show about a child beauty pageant contestant and her "trailer trash" family was poignant in that Parton surely understands the exploitation at work in such entertainment. Like the little girl, she has been the punch line of late-night talk-show jokes. But Honey Boo Boo had no choice and, to some extent, the family that was offered a much-needed check from the TLC network didn't either.

More successful than Parton referencing hip-hop is hip-hop referencing her. Minaj, for instance, twerks while she dares you to degrade her, calls out Parton's goddaughter Miley Cyrus for cultural appropriation, and makes sure her curves are in your face while she does it. She ends a rap appearance on the Drake song "Make Me Proud" with a direct invocation: "Double D up, hoes. Dolly Parton."

GOD'S LITTLE DOLLY PARTON

Part of Parton's power as a woman is that she has preserved something of the little girl she once was, not just as the main character in a song about a coat sewn from rags but in her abiding sense of wonder about the world.

In one of the more startling passages of her autobiography, *Dolly: My Life and Other Unfinished Business*, Parton describes a primal joy about the natural world.

"Sometimes I like to run naked in the moonlight and the wind, on the little trail behind our house, when the honeysuckle blooms," Parton wrote. "It's a feeling of freedom, so close to God and nature."

One might find this claim fantastical and dubious in other celebrity memoirs, but Parton has only described what she once knew as a child: the feral liberty of the poor child whose parents are hard at work while she entertains herself. Parton's rural upbringing, as well as the talent that set her apart from other kids, meant that her closest friend was the Earth itself. It's easy to believe that an icon known for her groundedness has been re-creating that experience on a trail through her Tennessee compound.

"The full moon is my best time," Parton wrote. "It's a good feeling to have no makeup, no wig, no high heels, just my little stubby self. Just God's little Dolly Parton again."

Simultaneous with Parton's Christian faith, this is the spirituality—erotic, embodied, without need of man or dogma—that has been with Parton since her early days. In *Dolly*, she counted three loves that most shaped her: God, music, and sex. They are all evident in her rural East Tennessee beginnings—the harsh Pentecostal faith of her pastor grandfather, the homemade instruments she played barefoot on porches, the twelve children her mother bore presumably for lack of birth control and need of farm help.

Parton, like her creative mother with a box of rags, has refashioned and sewn these themes together to create her own authentic life. While building a career on music, Parton claimed sexual power—not just in relationship to a partner but in relationship to the entire world—and carried herself with a faith that expresses itself through Christianity but finds its power within rather than without. ("The magic is inside you," Parton has said. "There ain't no crystal ball.")

In her autobiography, Parton mused about creating a line of high-quality bras for large-chested women, because she loved lingerie and found it lacking in her size. Her next thought is a loving kiss-off to the pastor grandfather who, when she was a teenager, shamed her as a harlot for wearing makeup and tight clothes. "Grandpa Jake is in heaven now," she wrote. "I hope he's getting a kick out of seeing me go into business hawking the very things he used to chastise me for."

In constructing the story of her life through interviews, live performances, books, and autobiographical TV movies, Parton has masterfully forced the world to reckon with that which patriarchy tries to conceal.

In the seminal 1992 feminist book *Women Who Run with*

the Wolves: Myths and Stories of the Wild Woman Archetype, Clarissa Pinkola Estés exhumed an archetype she said had been deliberately removed from myths, religious stories, and culture.

"This is how many women's teaching tales about sex, love, money, marriage, birthing, death, and transformation were lost," Estés wrote. ". . . Most old collections of fairy tales and mythos existent today have been scoured clean of the scatological, the sexual, the perverse (as in warnings against), the pre-Christian, the feminine, the Goddesses, the initiatory, the medicines for various psychological malaises, and the directions for spiritual raptures."

The "Wild Woman," Estés wrote, can be found again through new stories, art, and community.

"As a child, I was lucky to be surrounded by people from many of the old European countries and Mexico. . . . They, and many others—Native Americans, people from Appalachia, Asian immigrants, and many African-American families from the South—came to farm, to pick, to work in the ash pits and steel mills, the breweries, and in domestic jobs. Most were not educated in the academic sense, yet they were intensely wise. They were the bearers of a valuable and almost pure oral tradition."

The removal of women from country radio by male executives is but an echo of the removal of female stories from foundational and historical texts. Neither, we see from Parton's songwriting, life, and career, can stop a woman from being heard. She is a modern-day emblem of the wayward woman, the Wild Woman of myth and feminist texts.

That woman was in full glory during the 1989 Country Music Awards. Parton performed the Don Francisco gospel song "He's Alive," which she covered on that year's *White Limozeen* album after being moved by the song when she heard it one night on her tour bus. At the CMA performance, alone onstage, a tight white gown covered her from neck to wrist to ankle but clung to her curves. Her big blond wig and shiny red lips were not the stuff of modesty.

The song tells the story of Jesus's resurrection through the eyes of Peter, who initially doesn't believe the first person to see Jesus alive after his tomb was found empty—the female apostle Mary Magdalene. He and John find the tomb empty, as Mary had said, but believe his body has been taken by authorities.

At the CMAs, Parton sang the story with trepidation in her voice and on her face, her head cocked and eyes a bit glazed, like she was channeling the song from somewhere else. Eventually, as goes the Bible tale, Peter sees the resurrected Jesus with his own eyes and is overwhelmed with a sense of peace, joy, and release. At that, a bridge changed the key of the song.

Parton conveyed the epiphany by turning toward the back of the stage and lifting her arms. As she did so, a stage-wide screen behind her was supposed to rise, apparently. But there was some sort of technical delay, it seemed, and Parton turned back to the microphone to begin the triumphant breakthrough verse with her clear, booming pipes: "He's alive!" As she did, the screen finally came up, revealing a large choir in angelic robes who echoed "He's alive" higher on the scale.

I haven't belonged to the Christian faith in many years, but watching the old performance online gave me goosebumps and nearly brought me to tears—not for the religion in it but for the transcendent accomplishment of the song, the voices, the woman at the front of the stage in utter command, possessed by her own performance.

The song so thoroughly destroyed the auditorium full of country music performers that, as the camera panned to the crowd, at least one older man could be seen weeping.

There was a moment, then, when Parton seemed to realize what had just happened. Her eyes became clear and focused on the crowd, and her face took on a satisfied look that appeared to say, "Welp, we just brought this bitch down." Before thanking the choir, she swaggered backward with a swing in her hips. She had just accomplished her professional mission: to see God in a song and in the process let the whole world see her.

DON'T NEED NO COMPANY

Early in Dolly Parton's career, when her lifelong best friend, Judy, got out of the Air Force, the two took a trip to New York to live it up with Parton's new money from *The Porter Wagoner Show*. She was a country TV star but could still go relatively unrecognized in New York City, according to her book *Dolly*. The pair put on tight skirts and heavy makeup and went out on the town—each with a .38-caliber handgun in her purse. "I felt comfortable enough around a gun, and at that time I thought carrying one was the thing to do," Parton wrote.

New York was a grittier place then, around 1970, and they were twenty-something country girls on a mission: to be bad. They found a seedy movie theater and settled in to watch a porn. This attempt at a bit of harmless scandal turned out to be uncomfortable, though—two young women in a bad-smelling theater with a handful of men who were "the raincoat type." The movie itself disturbed them. "What we thought would be exciting and sexy was gross, filthy, and insulting," Parton wrote. She and Judy walked out.

A few blocks down the street, according to the book, they leaned against a wall—"dressed the way we were"—to collect themselves. A drunk man asked Parton for her rate as a prostitute. She told him to get lost. "We don't need no company," Parton remembered saying.

In response, he assaulted her—"grabbing at me in places I reserve for grabbers of my own choosing"—and telling her she wanted it. Parton pulled her Smith & Wesson out of her purse, and he left. "I could hear him calling me a bitch as he walked away," she wrote.

Half a century later, Parton is as big a star in New York and around the world as in Nashville, and her entourage carries the guns. The parable, though, endures. "Am I asking for it?" she has challenged society with her empowered carriage and provocative appearance ever since.

Parton learned early what people would see when they looked at her—a cheap woman whose appearance and sexuality warranted more immediate attention than her work. As she has said onstage, her mother used to tell her, "I hope you get a blessing out of it." That's exactly what Parton did with the unfortunate assignment society handed her.

She is thus a woman of paradoxes: Someone who acts "trashy" and has more class than most. Someone who dresses "like a hooker" and is a family-oriented, self-proclaimed homebody. A giggly blonde who is smarter than her male employees. A little girl who "got out" by singing about the place she left. A Christian who acts like, well, a true Christian. A woman of extraordinary depth who came into the world named after a toy doll—a term of endearment that also suggests an inhuman object created for someone else's pleasure.

"If I got any charm at all, it's that I look totally phony, but I am totally real," Parton told *Cineaste* in 1990. "That's my magic."

She is a rare sort of icon—at once a sex symbol like Marilyn Monroe, a creative genius like Loretta Lynn, and a philanthropic juggernaut like Oprah Winfrey. Meanwhile, Parton performs herself and, if she is a whore, well, she is also the pimp turning herself out and the john enjoying it.

"You spent good money on me," Parton told the crowd during one of her 2016 arena performances, as if to say that she remembered what it was to scrape together money for a night out. How could she forget? That was the theme of half the songs she sang.

The audience, as ever, appreciated her memories of lean times. The loudest applause came, however, when she asked whether she should run for president.

We likely will never see a presidential bust of Parton, but in 1987 her native Sevier County installed a life-sized bronze statue of her outside its downtown courthouse. In this representation, she is a young woman with her hair pulled back sitting on a rock with an acoustic guitar, her jeans cuffed at the ankles to reveal bare feet. This Parton is closer to the one who runs in the woods than the one who plays arenas in rhinestone-covered jumpsuits.

"After my dad died, one of my brothers told me that Daddy used to put a big oil drum of soapy water and a broom in the back of his truck," Parton told Jimmy Kimmel on his talk show in 2016. "And late at night he'd go down to the statue and scrub all the pigeon poop off."

Whatever sort of icon she is, whatever she represents to her fans and the rest of society—a wax sculpture wearing sequined shoulder pads in a Los Angeles museum of celebrity likenesses, a barefoot bronze in East Tennessee, or a living national treasure who defies easy categories—Parton survived and even changed a man's world so brilliantly that one occasionally sees on T-shirts or online memes an unlikely reference to perhaps the most powerful, least political feminist in the world. It's a line that, Parton recalled on Kimmel, her own father had on a bumper sticker on his pickup: "Dolly Parton for president."

ACKNOWLEDGMENTS

Thank you to my editor, Kathryn Belden, for deciding this writing should become a book and expertly leading the process; my literary agent, Julie Barer, for being on my side for six years now; and my publicist, Kate Lloyd, for sending my work into the world with gusto and sensitivity. I am fortunate to be on this powerful, reliable team.

Thank you to the many talented people at Scribner and Simon & Schuster who continue to believe in my voice and who made this book a reality.

Thank you to *No Depression* magazine, which published an earlier form of these contents as a quarterly series over the course of 2017; the FreshGrass Foundation, which funded the effort; and Kim Ruehl, former editor in chief of *No Depression*. Thank you to those who advocated for that project, including Allison Moorer, Anna DeVries, and Manjula Martin.

Thank you to booksellers large and small, especially independent bookstores who have cheered my writing within intimate communities while providing safe spaces for ideas and discussion. Thank you to the Kansas queen of them, Sarah Bagby at Watermark Books, for being a friend and champion.

Thank you to Dolly Parton for her unique cultural presence, onto which people around the world project a million ideas that reveal more about themselves than about her. I have speculated about Ms. Parton's motives and analyzed her life through the lens of my own experiences: as a Kansas farm kid born to a teenage mother in poverty, as a young woman who hustled tips as a "Hooters Girl," and as a first-generation college graduate who went on to inhabit academic and activist circles. My resulting insights about gender, place, and class are not meant to impose unwanted labels or presume to know the truths that Ms. Parton alone possesses.

Thank you to all the women of Ms. Parton's generation, including those whose political frameworks differ from my own.

Thank you to my family for yet again giving their blessing to share details of our private past in the interest of illuminating a broader history. Thank you to my mother, a lover of country music who once asked me, when I was a child, whether I thought the melody or lyrics mattered more. She added, "For me, it's the lyrics"; indeed, her affinity with language made me a writer. Thanks especially to the real Dolly Parton, my grandmother Betty.

It was not intentional, but all the people named here are female. Along my professional and creative path, nearly every person who saw my true value, and advanced me from difficult beginnings to a happy and abundant present, was a woman.

ABOUT THE AUTHOR

SARAH SMARSH is a journalist who has reported for the *New York Times*, the *Guardian*, and many other publications. Her first book, *Heartland: A Memoir of Working Hard and Being Broke in the Richest Country on Earth*, was a finalist for the National Book Award. A 2018 research fellow at Harvard University's Shorenstein Center on Media, Politics and Public Policy, Smarsh is a frequent speaker and commentator on economic inequality. She lives in Kansas.